ARMS AND ARMOUR OF
THE ENGLISH CIVIL WARS

Keith Dowen

CONTENTS

INTRODUCTION...........................3

CIVIL WAR ARMIES 5

ARMS AND ARMOUR IN ART.......6

ARMOUR...................................10
  Cuirassier's Armour 12
  Harquebusier's Armour................21
  Pikemen's Armour.......................30
  Buff Coats.................................39

FIREARMS 44
  Muskets 46
  Pistols and Carbines....................58

SWORDS....................................68
  Rapiers......................................72
  Hangers 74
  Basket Hilts...............................76

STAFF WEAPONS...........................80
  Pikes 81
  Halberds, Partizans
    and Leading Staffs....................84
  Pollaxes and Bills 87
  Lochaber Axes
    and Jedburgh Staves..................90
  Lances.......................................91

CONCLUSION...............................92

GLOSSARY 94

FURTHER READING.....................95

NOTES ON CURRENCY
AND DATES 95

ACKNOWLEDGEMENTS.............96

Front cover: Detail of a high-quality rapier with English hilt and Italian blade, *c.*1620-30. IX.883

Page 1: An early harquebusier's pott, *c.*1640 IV.375

▶ Hilt of a mid-17th century hanger with a brass pommel in the form of a lion's head. IX.760

Back cover: German wheellock pistol, *c.*1640. XII.1815

INTRODUCTION

The Civil Wars of the mid 17th century tore families and friendships apart, setting father against son and brother against brother. It pitted the Crown against Parliament in a struggle lasting more than a decade, and led to the execution of King Charles I on a chilly January morning in 1649. Yet the tragedy of the Civil Wars was not confined to England and Wales. It encompassed the whole of Britain and Ireland and even touched the nascent American colonies. Many European powers – France, Spain and the Dutch Republic, to name three – supplied arms and money, whilst foreign soldiers and engineers entered the service of both King and Parliament. As such there is no agreed title for the conflict: it has been variously called 'the English Civil War', 'the Great Rebellion', 'the Wars of the Three Kingdoms' and 'the British Civil Wars'. Nor was there a single war of which to speak, but rather a series of local and regional conflicts that began with the First Bishops' War in 1639 and ended with the Cromwellian conquest of Ireland in 1653.

Prior to the Civil Wars, Britain enjoyed a lengthy period of relative peace, and at first the native arms industry was ill-prepared to meet the demands of a large-scale conflict. With the outbreak of hostilities the main royal magazines and militia stores were targeted as commanders sought to equip their men. Although all sides relied on native arms producers, the scale of the conflict forced them to look abroad for military supplies. This was especially true for the Scots and Irish whose arms industries were significantly smaller than that in England.

The study of arms and armour, as with all material culture, largely depends on surviving pieces. Happily, more Civil War-era arms and armour survives than in any preceding period in British history. However there are still many gaps in our knowledge. Little is known about arms manufacturing outside London, for example; even less in Scotland and Ireland. Fortunately the abundance of military manuals, eyewitness accounts, official documents, newssheets and works of art offer invaluable alternative insights. This book introduces the types of arms and armour commonly found on Civil War battlefields, and places them within a larger framework that explains not only their design, but also their production, supply and use.

CIVIL WAR ARMIES

Civil War armies were composed of cavalry and infantry, which at the time were usually termed 'horse' and 'foot'. Although there was no standard model, the cavalry were organised into regiments, each of which was usually divided into six troops under the command of a colonel. Each troop consisted of between 30 and 100 men, the vast majority of whom were armed as harquebusiers (see pages 27-29 and 40), and was commanded by a captain. Whilst charismatic commanders such as Oliver Cromwell and Prince Rupert were able to attract large numbers of recruits, others were less fortunate: Colonel John Dalbier, for example, whose Parliamentarian regiment comprised four troops in 1644, led just 43 officers and 267 men. Due to the problem of procuring suitable horses, Scottish cavalry units were often quite small, sometimes comprising just two or three troops.

Like the cavalry, the infantry of the Civil Wars was organised into regiments, each of which was usually divided into ten or twelve companies under the command of a colonel. Regiments varied in size but would ideally contain around 1,200 men. Each company was commanded by field officers and was composed of musketeers and pikemen. The preferred ratio of musketeers to pikemen was two to one, although this was entirely dependent on the company having sufficient firearms. In his 'Observations on Military and Political Affairs', General George Monck advocated an equal ratio of pikemen to musketeers to ensure adequate protection for the latter. Some regiments, like the Marquis of Montrose's Irish Brigade, completely dispensed with the pike.

◀ Detail from a plan of the battle of Naseby (1645) by Robert Streeter (1624-80) published in Joshua Sprigg's *Anglia Rediviva* (1647).

CIVIL WAR ARMS AND ARMOUR IN ART

Although falling between the eras of the two great 17th-century artists Sir Anthony van Dyke (1599-1641) and Sir Peter Lely (1618-80), the period of the Civil Wars is nonetheless rich in portraits of the main protagonists. Two English artists in particular stand out: Robert Walker (*c*.1599-1658, see page 92), who painted many of the leading Parliamentarians, and William Dobson (1611-46), who became 'court painter' to the Royalists at Oxford. Unlike the grand portraiture of the nobility produced prior to the Wars, contemporary events gave rise to a new class of military patron. These men wished to be shown not as courtiers but soldiers, with arms and armour taking a prominent position in the overall composition of the painting. Consequently the growing importance of firearms over edged weapons, for instance, is clearly reflected in the portraiture of the period, particularly by William Dobson who lived and worked amongst intense military activity. Details of firearms and armour were rendered accurately, allowing aspects of style and construction to be clearly observed. Additionally the study of buff coats (see page 39), for example, is greatly aided by contemporary portraiture as so few coats have survived. Dobson also included many examples of Dutch armour in his portraits, accurately reflecting the importance (especially to the Royalists) of Continental imports.

Nonetheless, despite their usefulness, these portraits do have limitations. For example, it was Walker's habit, following on from van Dyke, to portray his sitters wearing full plate armour at a time when it was seldom worn on the battlefield. Its inclusion in portraits, therefore, was more symbolic than a reflection of reality. Armour was associated with the masculine, chivalric ideals of a romanticised past, and identified the sitter with their knightly forbears. Indeed, such was the symbolism of armour that as late as 1765 the artist Sir Joshua Reynolds painted the British commander in North America, Sir Geoffrey Amherst, in full plate.

In stark contrast to the rich variety of artistic sources produced on the Continent during the Thirty Years War (1618-48), one of the great limitations in understanding the arms and armour of the English Civil Wars is the lack of images depicting ordinary soldiers and the equipment they used. Although thousands of woodcut illustrations were produced, the depiction of arms and armour was often standardised. Cavalry troopers, for example, were frequently portrayed as fully-armoured cuirassiers, even though the vast

▶ An unidentified Royalist officer by William Dobson. © National Trust

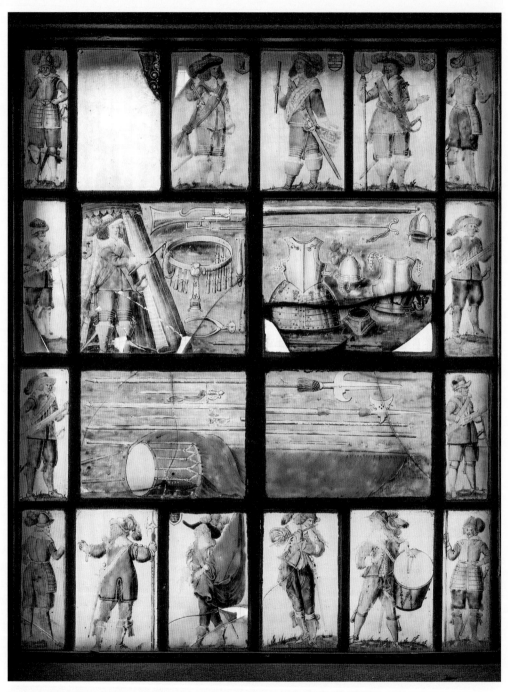

▲ A stained glass window in St Chad's Church, Farndon, Cheshire, depicting various soldiers and their equipment. © Mike Searle. Licensed under Creative Commons, CC-BY-SA.

majority of cavalrymen were equipped as harquebusiers. Probably the best known and most frequently-cited depiction of ordinary Civil War soldiers is the stained glass window in St Chad's Church, Farndon, Cheshire. It appears to have been commissioned between 1660 and 1663 by William Barnston, a captain in the regiment of Sir Francis Gamul, to commemorate his role and those of his fellow Royalists in the siege of Chester. However, far from accurately depicting the equipment and clothing styles of English soldiers during the 1640s, let alone the soldiers of Gamul's regiment, the figures are all largely based on earlier Continental sources. The sergeant, ensign, fifer and drummer along the bottom row, for example, are all inspired by the French artist Abraham Bosse (1602-72), who produced a series of etchings in the 1630s and early 1640s. In addition, whilst not a precise copy, the depiction of the panoply of musketeer and pikemen's arms in the central window panel was clearly based on a plate of Johann Jacobi von Walhausen's *Kriegskunst zu Fuss* (1615) and later reproduced with modifications by Henry Hexham.

The window in Farndon is by far the largest and most interesting example of a Cheshire-based industry producing stained glass that portrayed martial subjects taken from military manuals. Another well-preserved example at Poole Hall in Cheshire depicts the various postures of pike and musket. The 'Painted Room' in Clifton Hall in Nottinghamshire likewise possesses a collection of very fine panel paintings depicting 17th-century soldiers. Once again though, they are faithfully based on works by de Gheyn, and do not accurately represent contemporary English soldiers.

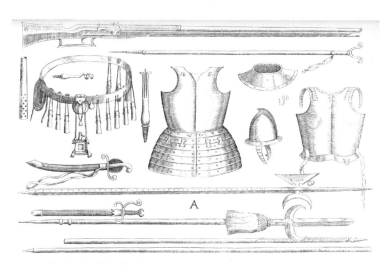

▲ Arms and armour as depicted in Johann Jacobi von Walhausen's *Kriegskunst zu Fuss* (1615).

▲ Pikeman from Henry Hexham's *Principles of the art military* (1637).

COLL ALEXANDER POPHAM.

ARMOUR

During the Civil Wars the vast majority of armour made in Britain was produced by the Armourer's Company of London, which had been granted its first charter by Henry VI in 1453. Although armourers were resident in many British towns and cities, they were primarily employed to maintain and repair existing stores of arms and armour rather than produce new pieces. Indeed, there appears to have been a dearth of properly trained armourers outside London. In January 1639, for example, it was reported that not only were the pikemen's corslets stored in Durham lacking tassets, but there was no-one in the town or county able to make them.

Parliament's control of London and subsequent seizure of the nation's major arsenals at the Tower of London and Hull certainly gave them an early advantage when it came to equipping their men with armour. However, many of the London armourers had been initially tasked with refurbishing the equipment deposited in the Committee of Safety's magazine. It is therefore perhaps not surprising that their initial output of new armour was low. As such, the first recorded bulk consignment of English-made armour was not until June 1643, until which time Parliament had to rely heavily on foreign imports.

The majority of armourers remained in London to serve Parliament. However, a small number, including Nicholas Sherman, who had been made 'Master of the Almains' at the Royal workshops at Greenwich in 1628, moved with the king to Oxford. Whilst an armoury had been established in the Schools Tower of the university its output appears to have been very low. Instead, the armourers spent most of their time repairing donated or captured armour. Although York had been developed as a manufacturing centre during the Bishops Wars, and Bristol was a recognized centre of arms producers, it is not clear how much armour they contributed to the Royalist war effort. Whilst the Royalists certainly obtained some of their armour abroad, their main concern was with equipping their men with weapons.

◄ Alexander Popham shown wearing a cuirassier armour. On the Civil War battlefield he is more likely to have worn a harquebusier's cuirass and buff coat. I.315

CUIRASSIER'S ARMOUR

▲ Cuirassier holding a wheellock pistol, with a second pistol sitting ready in its holster. © British Museum

Although many military theorists and commanders still valued the tactical role of the heavily armoured cavalryman, by 1600 more lightly armoured cavalry were moving into favour. Equipped with a range of short-barrelled flint- and wheellock firearms, and less encumbered by heavy armour, these light cavalrymen were eminently suited for a wide variety of roles. By the 1630s many Continental armies had dispensed with fully armoured cuirassiers as being both tactically less versatile and too costly to equip, although Britain, which had largely remained on the sidelines during recent events in Europe, continued to field fully armoured cuirassiers in the early years of the Civil Wars. However, by 1643/4 they too had become a rare sight.

The cost of cuirassier armour was particularly high. In 1632 the Lords Committees of the Council of War directed that the official price of cuirassier armour was £4 10s (roughly three times the cost of a harquebusier's armour). Cuirassier armour also took a long time to make. On 19 November 1639 the Armourer's Company reported the capacity to produce 800 pikemen's armours and 400 harquebusier's armours per month, but only 80 cuirassier's armours. One solution was to purchase armour abroad. In early 1639/40 the Council of War proposed ordering a large quantity of cuirassier armours with pistol-proof breastplates from Flanders (just over a month later 650 had been delivered). However, a cheaper and faster method of obtaining cuirassier armour was simply to refurbish old suits or even adapt 16th-century cavalry armours.

Due to the preponderance of firearms on the battlefield, many pieces of armour were made pistol- or carbine-proof. This effect was achieved by simply increasing the thickness of the plates, thereby making the armour heavier and more uncomfortable, and prompting men to discard certain

elements or even to refuse to wear the armour altogether. When Sir Edmund Verney, Knight Marshal of England, was summoned to serve as a cuirassier in the Bishops' Wars he famously replied that 'it will kill a man to serve in a whole cuirass. I am resolved therefore to use nothing but back breast and gauntlet; if I had a Pott for the Head that were Pistoll-proofe it mayee bee I would use it if it were light'.

▶ Dutch cuirassier armour with traces of gilding, c.1630, showing 'proof' marks on the breastplate and tassets. The entire armour weighs 39 kg. II.140

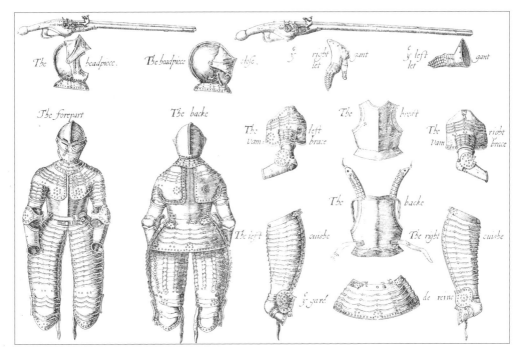

The following labels appear within the illustration:

The headpiece.   *The headpiece close*.   *y right let gant*   *y left let gant*

The forepart   *The backe*   *The Vam left brace*   *The brest*   *The Vam right brace*

The left cuishe   *The backe*   *The right cuishe*

y gard   *de reine*

▲ Cuirassier equipment depicted in John Bingham's *Tactics of Aelian* (1616).

In 1642 the Royalist captain Henry Hexham noted in his *Principles of the Art Military* that cuirassiers were equipped with a pistol-proof helmet, a gorget, breast and back plates ('ideally pistol-proofe'), a pair of pauldrons and vambraces, a culet or 'gard de reines', a pair of gauntlets and a pair of knee-length tassets. Although not mentioned by Hexham, other writers recommended cuirassiers wore a buff coat to protect the body 'from the pinching of his ponderous armour'. How far this ideal reflected actual practice is not always clear.

Whilst most contemporary military manuals depicted cuirassiers wearing close helmets, by the 1630s this was being increasingly replaced by the lighter 'close burgonet' which provided better ventilation and all-round visibility. Constructed in a very similar manner to the close helmet, the distinguishing feature of the close burgonet was the pivoted projecting peak, or fall. One common style of face-guard incorporated a series of long vertical bars directly attached to the peak. Another, the 'Todenkopf' or 'Death's Head' helmet, featured a face-guard in the form of a face or skull. By the mid 1630s, both artistic and literary evidence indicates that growing numbers of cuirassiers were dispensing with close-helmets altogether and instead equipping themselves with the lightweight *zischägge*, or pott.

▲ Dutch cuirassier's close helmet,
c.1635. IV.1026

▶ Death's Head, or 'Savoyard', close
helmet, c.1620. IV.48

▲ Cuirassier wearing long leather riding boots. Circle of van Dyke, *c*.1650. © Harvard College

▶ Gilt Dutch cuirassier armour of Charles I, originally made for his elder brother Henry, Prince of Wales. Unusually, the armour incorporated plate greaves and sabatons. II.91

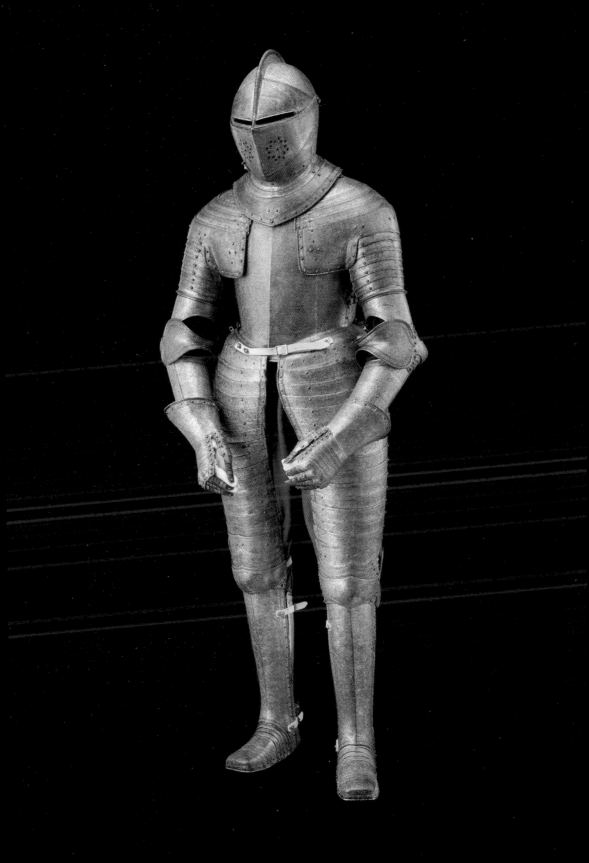

The short-waisted breastplate, some of which were pistol-proof, incorporated a flange at the base for the attachment of the tassets. A corresponding flange on the backplate enabled the attachment of the culet, or garde de reins, which protected the lower back and buttocks. The culet could either take the form of a short skirt formed of narrow horizontal lames or, in the Eastern European style, a series of metal scales riveted to a leather backing. The front of the legs were protected by a pair of long laminated tassets which extended from the waist to the knee. From the late 16th century the wearing of greaves and sabatons had become increasingly rare (although they were sometimes included with higher quality armours) with the lower legs instead protected by stout leather riding boots. Many tassets were formed of two or three sections which allowed the wearer to shorten them if required. The vambraces were usually made with the upper and lower arms permanently joined together, however, some allowed the lower part to be removed by the provision of a slot and turning pin located between the shoulder and elbow. As an additional protective measure some Continental armours incorporated a series of narrow articulating lames, or splints, which protected the inner bend of the elbows.

With functionality often being the overriding factor, decoration on most cuirassier armour was generally kept to a minimum – usually single-, double-

◀ Very high-quality blued and gilt Flemish *zischägge* with red velvet lining. IV.587

▶ Portrait of George Digby, Earl of Bristol, in black or blued armour with gilt details. Justus van Egmont, *c*.1653. I.982

▲ Cavalry battle between harquebusiers, *c*.1645, by Pieter Meulener. © Netherlands Institute for Art History

or triple-incised lines around the edges of the plates. Gilding, where present, was restricted to rivet heads, swivel hooks, pierced studs and plume holders. On some high-quality Dutch and Flemish armours decoration was much more extensive with bands of etched and gilt decoration. Most armour of the period if not left rough and 'black from the hammer' was blackened to produce a striking (if sombre) appearance that also deterred corrosion. Armour could also be provided with a russet or reddish-brown finish: in 1639, for example, at the outbreak of the Bishops' Wars, King Charles summoned England's leading nobles and gentlemen to serve as cuirassiers 'in russet arms with gilded studs or nayles'. Finally, blueing was another surface finish applied to cuirassier,s armour. This more complex and costly method involved evenly heating the individual plates to achieve the desired deep peacock-blue colouration.

Despite its limitations, the protection offered by full armour could be considerable. At the battle of Roundway Down (1643) the fully-armoured Sir Arthur Haselrigge was repeatedly assailed by Captain Richard Atkyns of Prince Maurice's regiment. Although Atkyns discharged his pistols when he felt their barrels touch his opponent's armour, 'he was too well armed all over for a pistol bullet to do him any hurt'. Perhaps unsurprisingly Haselrigge was lampooned by the Royalists in the *Ballad of Runaway Down* as 'armed from his head to his arse in a hundredweight of iron'.

Named after the harquebus with which they were originally armed, the harquebusier had become the dominant type of cavalryman in Britain. Unlike the more heavily armoured cuirassier, the harquebusier's equipment was ideally suited to an offensive role requiring increased mobility and tactical flexibility. Indeed, the Parliamentarian officer John Vernon observed that 'The Harbuyusers and Carbines arming is chiefly offensive, his defensive Arms, are only an open Caske or Head-peece, a back and brest with a buffe coat under his armes'.

From the outset Parliament aimed to provide its cavalry with sufficient arms and armour. For example, in July 1642 the Committee of Lords and Commons for the Safety of the Kingdom ordered that each troop commander should be provided with £280 to cover the expense of mounting and arming their men. Following the establishment of the New Model Army in 1645, in addition to the armour already in service, Parliament contracted numerous London armourers to supply its forces with 500 complete cavalry armours and 400 additional helmets. Similarly, during the Scottish campaigns, London armourers again supplied large quantities of armour. As a result of the high production, the price of harquebusiers' armour fell over the course of the Civil Wars, from 20s in 1645 to only 16s by 1654.

◀ A horseman's helmet or 'caske', early 17th century. © Glasgow Museums Collection

However, not all harquebusiers were so well equipped. This appears to have been especially true of the Royalists, who relied heavily on individual donations and the stores of the county militias. As such, according to the Oxford 'Articles of War' published in 1644, a Royalist cavalryman could 'pass muster' even if he was only armed with a sword. The problem of supplying the Royalist horse at the beginning of the Civil Wars was noted by the Earl of Clarendon who reported that apart from the old backs, breasts and potts procured by the officers, the rest of the cavalry were poorly armed. Some troops were more successful in obtaining arms. In early 1643 Captain Richard Atkyns' troop of 60 harquebusiers was provided with '30 steel backs, breasts and head pieces' by the Gloucestershire Royalist Master, John Dutton. However, this was certainly not universal. Although the Royalists imported armour from the Netherlands they also relied on Scandinavian countries to furnish them with military supplies. The quality of these armours varied widely as arms dealers sought to profit in a fertile market.

There is comparatively little evidence for the widespread use of armour by Scottish cavalry, and among the Irish Confederates cavalry armour was virtually non-existent. In 1644 the Confederate Earl of Castlehaven was forced to obtain armour from Wexford to arm the first two ranks of his horse, which had been defenceless against the Scottish lancers.

▼ Early English harquebusier's pott or burgonet, c.1625. The holes around the outer edges are for the attachment of a lining. IV.159

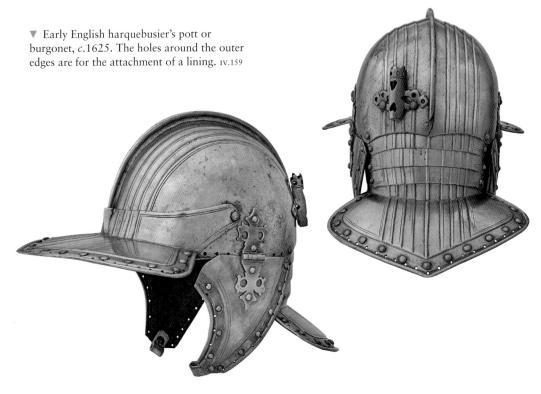

◀ Dutch harquebusiers pott with single nasal, *c*.1640. IV.174

▼ Harquebusier's pott, with a downward sloping brim, made in *c*.1645 by the London armourers Boulter and Keene. IV.547

Despite frequent references to 'open caskes' in contemporary military manuals, the most popular type of helmet was undoubtedly the pott, sometimes termed a 'headpiece'. Early harquebusiers' potts dating to the 1620s and early 1630s were notable for incorporating embossed and incised designs and were probably made at the same time as a series of London-made pikemens' corslets which shared many of the same features (pages 34-36). Possibly as a result of long-standing military ties with the Dutch Republic, the mid 1630s saw the introduction of a new style of helmet based on the Continental *zischägge*. Known today as a 'lobster pot', due to resemblance of the tail or neck guard to a lobster's tail, the helmet incorporated a triple-bar face-guard attached to the peak. Whilst similar examples were produced on the Continent, these do appear to have been particularly popular in England. In July 1645, for example, Parliament contracted London armourer Edward Barker for 'two hundred potts with three barres English at vii *s* a peece'. The earliest English potts incorporated laminated neckguards, although by the early 1640s their design had been greatly simplified – presumably due to the need to produce large numbers both affordably and easily. The most notable change was in the form of the neck-guard which was subsequently made from a single plate and embossed to simulate the separate lames. By the late 1640s considerable numbers of harquebusiers' potts were being contracted out to London armourers by Parliament for a set price. To meet demand the design of the pott was further simplified, with all extraneous decoration removed. Older potts, however, were often recycled with elements incorporated into later helmets.

Continental *zischägges*, which had developed from the Ottoman çiçak, were also worn during the Civil Wars, particularly by Royalist, Scottish and Irish cavalry who relied most heavily on foreign imports. Due to the shortage of suitable helmets when war broke out, older helmets, such as 15th-century sallets, were sometimes modified into harquebusier potts by the addition of peaks, neck-guards and face-guards.

◀ 15th-century sallet converted into a harquebusier's pott with the addition of a peak, *c.*1642. IV.8

▲ Flemish *zischägge* with characteristic ribbed helmet bowl, *c.*1630. IV.907

▶ Comparison between an early harquebusier's pott, *c.*1640 (exhibiting a deeper bowl and more refined peak, but missing its cheekpieces), and a later pott made during the Commonwealth. IV.375, 894

The term 'steel cap' or 'steel bonnet' occasionally appears in Scottish sources of the period. On 18 August 1643, for instance, the cavalry of the Army of the Solemn League and Covenant were ordered to appear at Leith wearing steel caps, or bonnets, and secrets. References to steel bonnets can be found from the late 15th century and appear to refer to any metal helmet, worn both by infantry and cavalry, not necessarily a specific type. The 'secret', on the other hand, was a metal skull cap worn beneath a felt or woollen hat which was designed to protect the wearer against sword cuts. In some instances a metal framework was incorporated into the construction of the hat. Charles I, for example, is recorded as having worn a steel cap covered with velvet at the battle of Edgehill in 1642.

The early harquebusier breastplates of the 1630s featured a fashionable dipped waistline or residual peascod shape. However, from the early 1640s the waistline became less exaggerated and the residual peascod reduced to a simple point. Until the mid 1640s gorgets were sometimes issued alongside back and breastplates. Nonetheless, this was not universal practice, presumably as the high neckline found on most breastplates obviated their need. Back and breastplates were simply secured with a leather waist-belt and a pair of plated shoulder straps. Earlier breastplates frequently incorporated swivel hooks mounted on decorative quatrefoil washers. However, by the early 1640s this extraneous detail was omitted, and mushroom-headed studs, which engaged with keyhole slots on the terminal plates of the shoulder straps, were attached to the breastplate. In contrast, the shoulder straps on Dutch armour were usually secured to the breastplate with pierced studs and small swivel hooks.

The bullet-dents seen on many breastplates are not usually the result of battle damage, but from 'proofing' or testing the armour against pistol or caliver shot. This was often undertaken by the armourer prior to the final finishing. In some cases, though, the armourer deliberately undercharged the firearm in order to deceive the buyer. Apart from making armour thicker, another way in which armourers responded to the need for shot-proof armour was simply to join an old and a newly-made breastplate (and sometimes backplates) together. This could be achieved either by simply folding the edges together, forge-welding or riveting to produce a so-called 'duplex' or multi-layered armour.

During the Civil Wars, plate elbow (or bridle) gauntlets were worn to protect the vulnerable lower left arm. Only ever worn in limited numbers, by the mid 1640s they appear to have largely fallen out of use. In addition to plate gauntlets, a variety of styles of buff leather gauntlets were also worn.

▼ Harquebusier's armour traditionally associated with Colonel Alexander Popham, *c.*1630, from the armoury at Littlecote House. III.1956A, 1957, 1958

▶ Detail of the decorative swivel hook and washer.

◄ High-waisted English cuirass exhibiting a bullet dent, *c*.1650. III.1976

▼ Bridle gauntlet, mid 17th century. III.1476

▶ Portrait of Royalist officer Sir Jacob Astley (1579-1652) wearing an early English harquebusier's cuirass over a gorget. Attributed to Adriaen Hanneman. Philip Mould & Company

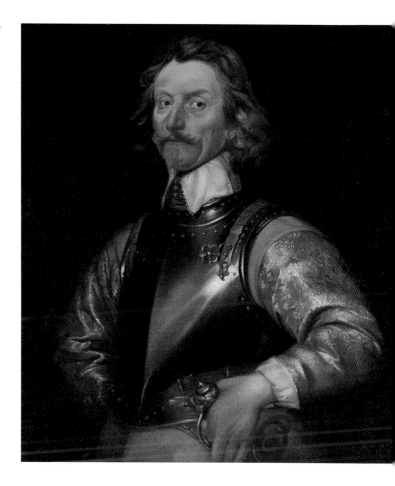

▽ A pair of buff leather gauntlets from the armoury at Littlecote House, c.1650.
III.1956b, 1956c

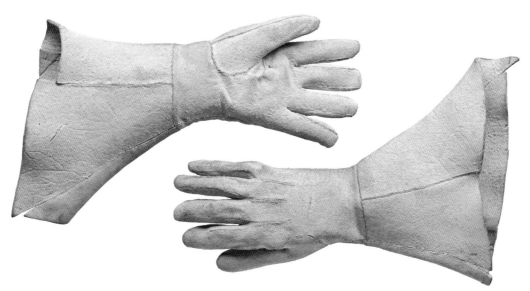

PIKEMEN'S ARMOUR

Prior to the 17th century many pikemen had been heavily armed with half-armours, known as corselets, which comprised a helmet, gorget, pauldrons, vambraces, gauntlets, back and breast plates and a pair of tassets. However, by the reign of Charles I this had been significantly reduced. As early as 1590 John Smythe had complained in his *Certain Discours* that pikemen only wore 'their burgonets their collars their cuirasses and their backs, without either pouldrons, vambraces, gauntlets or tasses'. Whilst armour was undoubtedly beneficial when engaged in 'push of pike', experience of war on the Continent taught how impractical it could be on long marches or when fighting in difficult terrain. One contemporary clearly sympathised with the predicament of armoured pikemen by noting that 'to be put upon long and quick Marches in hot Summer weather, with Armes compleat as well for Pike as for Corslet, cannot but be wonderfully

◀ A pikeman wearing a pott and cuirass with tassets, from *Wappenhandelinghe* by Jacob de Gheyn (1607).

▲ A rare depiction of a Dutch pikeman carrying his kit. By Jan Martszen de Jonge, *c.*1633. © Rijksmuseum

burthensome'. In 1639 the 'Directions for Musters' specified corselets were only to comprise 'a Gorget, Back, Breast, Tassets and Head-piece'.

There seems to have been a gradual decline in the wearing of armour by pikemen during the Civil Wars. On the whole, being in control of the nation's capital and with easier access to Continental markets, Parliament was better able to supply its pikemen with armour. In 1642, for instance, Parliament ordered 6000 corselets from France and the Netherlands. However, following the defeat of the Earl of Essex at the battle of Lostwithiel in September 1644 and the loss of the army's equipment, there appears to have been no attempt to resupply pikemen with armour. Additionally, there are no references to corselets among the contracts of supplies for the New Model Army in 1645 – although there may have already been sufficient stores in existence. As the New Model Army was formed from three separate armies, it is also possible that soldiers continued to wear the armour with which they had previously been issued. What these contracts do demonstrate, though, is that obtaining corselets was no longer a priority. Indeed there is no evidence for the Armourer's Company of London producing pikemen's armour after 1649.

◀ English pikeman's armour, c.1625, exhibiting extensive embossed and rivetted decoration reminiscent of Bargello 'Flame stitch'. II.269

▶ An unknown officer wearing a chevron-embossed breastplate over a buff coat, c.1640. © August Heckscher Collection

The Royalists, on the other hand, never appear to have been well supplied with pikemen's armour. Instead, they were forced to rely on what they could obtain from the stores of the county militias, much of which was in a poor state. Certainly at the start of the war in 1642, the Royalists were critically short of equipment, with the Earl of Clarendon famously remarking that 'in the whole body there was not one pikeman had a corselet'. By 1644 conditions in some regiments were no better, with Prince Rupert's regiment of foot being reported as 'very poor and ragged, very many had no arms but swords'.

The earliest identifiable group of English pikemen's armours, dating to the 1620s, incorporated extensive embossing, decorative copper-alloy rivets and elaborate hinge plates. The embossed decoration often took the form of long stepped chevrons, emulating contemporary 'flame stitch' or 'Bargello' needlework fabrics. It used to be thought that they were produced in the royal workshops of Greenwich, although the identification of a number of different London armourer's marks on several of them has disproved this hypothesis.

From the beginning of his reign Charles I had earnestly sought to improve the quality of the nation's militia and standardise military equipment. This appears to have been reflected in the design of London-made armour, which from the mid 1630s began to lose its elaborate details that were time-consuming and labour-intensive.

The pikeman's pott, otherwise known as a headpiece, was first developed in the Low Countries and had evolved out of the older morion and cabasset. As shown in the illustrations of Jacob de Gheyn and Adam van Breen, it typically comprised a relatively low-combed skull with a downward angled brim. As was common to all European helmets after 1600, the skull was made in two pieces, joined at either end of the brim by rivets, and hammer-welded closed along the comb. The lining, which filled the entire bowl and brim was sewn onto canvas or leather lining bands which were secured in place by rivets and washers. According to Gervase Markham the lining was usually made of buckram, though he personally advised using more comfortable 'strong huswives linnen' instead. The evolution of the pott from the 1620s to 1640s is rather complex, however English examples are notable for the size of their brims giving them a 'boat-like' appearance. In contrast, Dutch potts generally featured much shallower brims and had a much more 'compact' shape. As with most armour of the period decoration was kept to a minimum.

Alongside the pikeman's pott, cabassets (or 'Spanish morions' as they were known in England) continued to be worn in the early 1600s. Comprising an almond-shaped skull with a short backward-pointing 'stalk' at the apex and a narrow brim, cabassets were originally of one-piece construction, but from

◀ High quality Flemish pikeman's pott, formerly blued and gilt, *c*.1630. IV.1615

▼ Typical English 'boat-shaped' pikeman's pott, *c*.1630. IV.228

◀ A basic munition-quality Dutch pikeman's pott, *c*.1630. IV.920

▲ A typical English pikeman's pott, *c*.1635. II.337

◀ A munition-quality two-part cabasset riveted together along the ridge, early 17th century. IV.728

*c.*1600 were usually made in two halves. Other older styles of helmet, including medieval kettle-hats, were pressed into service as the need arose.

During the 1620s, pikemen's breastplates incorporated a marked residual peascod which in some cases took on a thin prow-like form. However, in the 1630s this feature was gradually reduced in size until it formed only a slight dip at the base of the breastplate. By contrast, the design of Dutch breastplates was more advanced, having lost the residual peascod much earlier in the century. In order to secure the tassets, the base of the breastplate incorporated a wide flange. Usually this was integral to the rest of the breastplate, though on some Continental examples the flange was made separately and riveted in place. In some cases breastplates incorporated a particularly deep flange in place of tassets. The back and breastplates were initially secured together by a pair of hinged or leather hasps riveted to the sides of the breastplates which fastened over pierced studs on the backplate. However, from around 1630 this was replaced with a waist-belt riveted to the backplate and buckled in front. Unlike harquebusier's armours, pikemen's corselets retained their pierced studs and swivel hooks. Gorgets were worn beneath the cuirass, not only to protect the neck, but also the spread the weight of the armour more evenly across the wearer's shoulders.

Originally tassets had been constructed from multiple overlapping lames held together on leathers and suspended from the breastplate by leather straps. Detachable multi-lame tassets continued in use for the first few decades of the 17th century, but by *c.*1620 many were instead made of single plates. Due to the frequency with which the leather straps broke or were cut, English tassets were initially held in place with pairs of ornate hinged hasps. However, during the 1630s and probably as a result of Dutch influence these were replaced by a much more basic design which were riveted permanently to the fauld of the breastplate. Not only did this simplify production, but it also prevented soldiers from easily removing and discarding them. Similar in design, though slightly smaller, Dutch tassets were usually attached to the breastplate with plated leather straps. In some cases these were re-fitted with English style hasps (presumably after they had been imported).

▶ French or Dutch breastplate, bearing the name 'TOIRAS' after the French Marshal Toiras, *c.*1627. III.205

◀ Dutch pikeman's
armour with
characteristic strap
and hook attachments
on the tassets, c.1630.
II.165

▶ A typical London-
made English
pikeman's armour,
c.1635. II.365

BUFF COATS

During the reign of Queen Elizabeth I, short waist-length leather coats or jerkins were often worn by soldiers in conjunction with, and in place of, plate armour. However, it was not until the 1610s, as plate armour became less popular, that the long-skirted buff coat was developed. During the 17th century the British leather industry was of significant economic importance: writer Henry Belasyse noted in 1657 that leather was one of the 'chief ryches' of the country. Indeed, in London and its suburbs alone there were over 6000 craftsmen working with leather at the beginning of the century. Originally produced from European buffalo hide, hence the name 'buff' coat, by the time of the Civil Wars most buff coats were made from other bovine or deer hides. In fact it is likely that the raiding of deer parks provided the required skins for these buff coats, as well as a wide range of military and civilian equipment. Buff coats were supplied to the armies by both leather-dressers and haberdashers. Humphrey Primate of the Company of Haberdashers, for example, who probably supplied officers throughout the Wars, provided 'buff coats and the like' valued at £40 10s to Colonel Audley Mervin, an officer serving in Ireland in 1646.

The extent to which buff coats were worn, particularly by harquebusiers, is not entirely clear. In 1661, in an addition to his 1635 book *The Young Artilleryman*, William Barriffe noted that during the Civil Wars harquebusiers had only been armed with breasts, backs and helmet (and many not even that). Similarly, not all military manuals listed buff coats among the harquebusier's essential equipment. It seems that many were purchased individually or provided by a regiment's colonel or home town, such as a troop of horse raised for Captain John Bird which was provided with 53 buff coats and 52 pairs of leather gauntlets by the Liberty of Watford. Parliament, once again, was in a better position to supply its forces: in July 1642, the Committee of Safety requested that the Committee for the Militia in London provide five hundred buff coats.

Contemporary sources indicate that officers regularly wore buff coats. In 1639 a letter from the Earl of Douglas noted that his friend Sir Thomas Hope 'will shortly bear his buff coat again as a commander at the wars'. Although primarily associated with the cavalry, buff coats were also worn by some infantrymen, particularly those of the militia, or 'Trained Bands'.

◀ Portrait of Royalist officer John Byron (1598/9-1652) wearing a plain buff coat with elaborately-decorated sleeves and hose. Painted by William Dobson, *c*.1642. © University of Manchester

◀ Harquebusier's
equipment at the time
of Cromwell's
campaigns in Scotland
and Ireland, *c*.1650.
III.1942, IV.547, IX.3356,
XIII.303

▶ Buff coat from
Littlecote House,
*c.*1650. III.1951

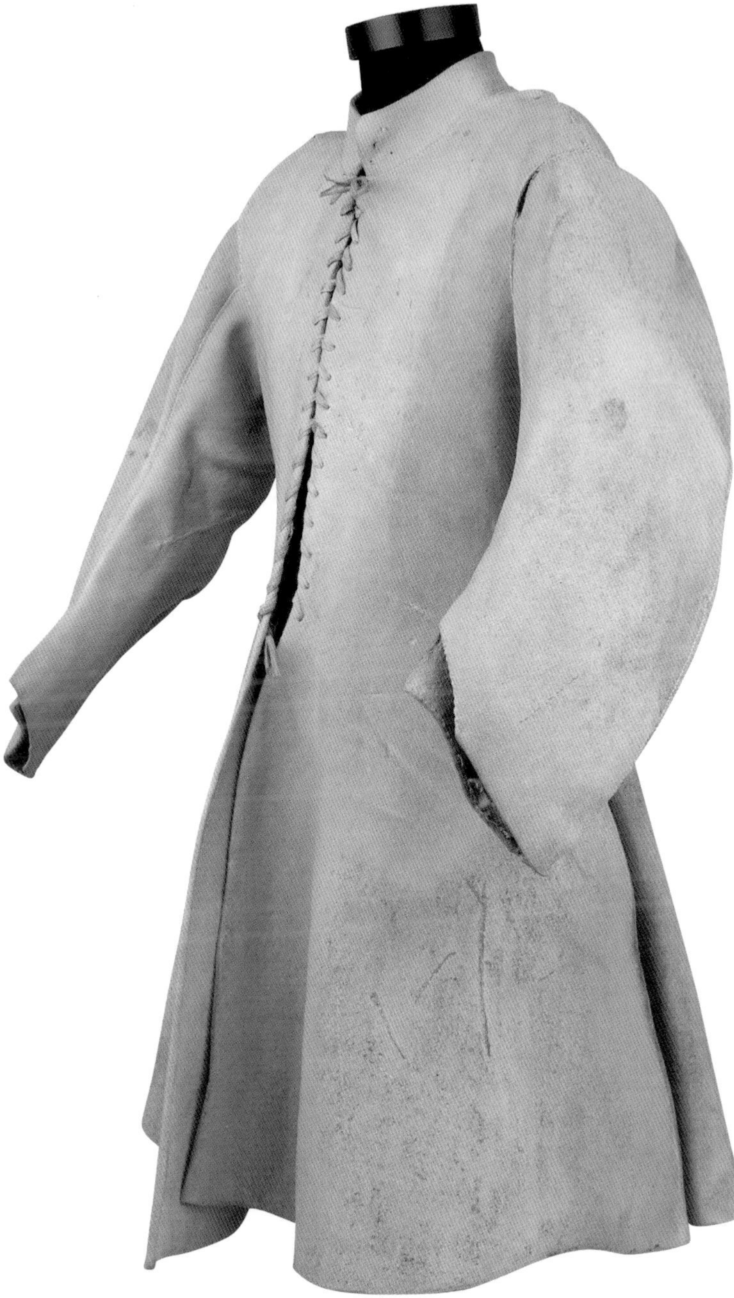

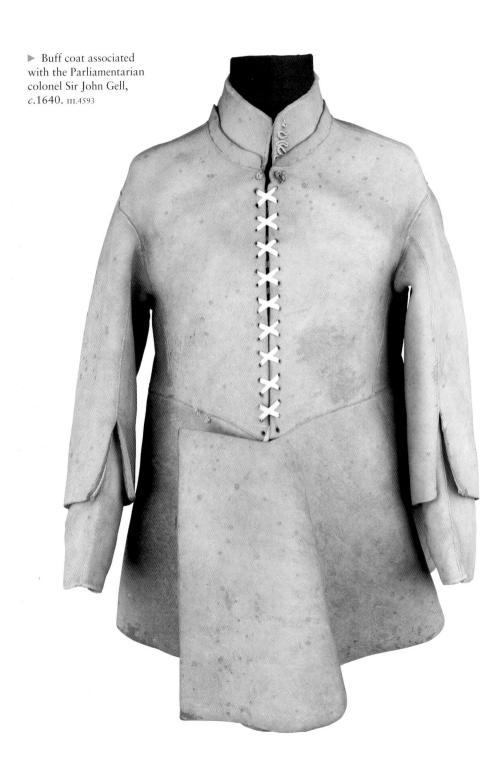

▶ Buff coat associated with the Parliamentarian colonel Sir John Gell, *c.*1640. III.4593

The Royalist news-sheet 'Mercurius Aulicus', for example, listed 'Trained Band Buff' among the spoils taken by the Royalists following the second battle of Newbury in 1644. However, these buff coats belonged to the London regiments, who were generally better equipped than most other Trained Bands. As a result it is not clear how common this practice was.

Often regarded as being expensive items, most ordinary trooper's buff coats appear to have cost between 30s and 40s, roughly double the price of a harquebusier's armour in 1640. Whilst a significant sum of money, they were nonetheless worn in sufficient numbers that the term 'Buffe Coate' was used in reference to a cavalry trooper at the Putney Debates in 1647. Of course expense would be influenced by complexity of design and any decorative embellishments.

During the 17th century, the design of buff coats closely followed civilian fashion, with many examples exhibiting close-fitting waists and flaring skirt panels. In the case of cavalry coats, long skirts were essential in covering the otherwise unarmoured upper leg. Buff coats could be constructed in a number of ways: some comprised two front and two back panels, whilst more complex examples incorporated multiple pieces that varied in thickness depending on the part of the body they were designed to cover. Buff coats were usually lined with linen, though more costly materials such as silk were available. Some were lined completely, but many only from the waist up. Buff coats appear in a range of colours from light grey to bright yellow ochre. Whilst these colours could be achieved through oxidation during production, buff coats could also be stained with ochre pigment. In order to maintain the bright yellow colour it may have been necessary to periodically re-apply the ochre stain.

Buff coats were fastened by a series of iron hooks and eyes sewn to the inner lining. A length of ribbon was then laced spirally down a line of holes pierced along the centre-front opening, with a second ribbon on the other side. Once the sides of the coat-front were fastened with the hidden hooks and eyes, the ribbons created an illusion of cross-lacing, and could be tied at the top and bottom to complete the effect. Button fastening was also used, though this method was much less widespread.

FIREARMS

British firearms production at the start of the Civil Wars slowly gathered pace. With London under its control Parliament had access to the Company of Gunmakers, which had been incorporated in 1637/38 – a significant development that overcame the problems caused by the division of work between blacksmiths and locksmiths. Despite this advantage, Parliament was, like the Royalists, still forced to purchase many of its firearms abroad. At the start of the war, London gunmakers spent much of their time simply refurbishing existing stock rather than producing new weapons. Nonetheless, by late 1643 they claimed to supply all of Parliament's needs, producing some 111,000 firearms between 1642 and 1651. Two remarkably industrious brothers, John and William Watson, are notable for having made 12,000 guns during the war. In all but the smallest workshops, labour was divided between craftsmen who made the barrels, locks and fittings, and 'stockers-up' who brought the components together to produce a finished piece.

Some of the London gunsmiths had moved with the king to Oxford, but in 1643 the capture of Bristol enabled the Royalists to utilise the various arms manufacturers in the city. Bristol was home to at least six gunmakers who produced 200 muskets a week. By 1645, just prior to its capture by Parliament, it was said that the city could furnish 15,000 muskets a year. However, demand continued to outstrip supply, and the Royalists were forced to rely heavily on foreign imports paid for by profits from the Cornish tin trade. Royalist privateers also intercepted Parliamentarian supply ships, but ultimately a lack of naval superiority was exposed: in November 1642, for example, Parliamentarian forces captured a Royalist vessel carrying 300 muskets and 500 cases of pistols from the Continent.

◄ Gunsmith at work, from a German Hausbuch (1613).

Developed by the middle of the 16th century, the most widely-used
infantry firearm during the Civil Wars was the matchlock musket.
The heaviest of all firearms on the battlefield, its long barrel and large bore
made it a powerful and effective weapon, particularly against armour.
Consequently, by the end of the 16th century, the matchlock musket was
replacing the lighter arquebus, or caliver, in European armies.

The earliest matchlock mechanisms had been developed at the start of the
15th century, and originally comprised a pivoted bar forming a serpentine,
or match-holder, at one end, with the other end functioning as a trigger lever.
When this lever was squeezed, the burning match was brought into contact
with the gunpowder in the priming pan which then ignited the main charge.
By the end of the century this simple mechanism had been largely replaced

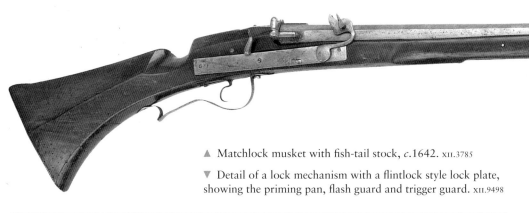

▲ Matchlock musket with fish-tail stock, c.1642. XII.3785

▼ Detail of a lock mechanism with a flintlock style lock plate,
showing the priming pan, flash guard and trigger guard. XII.9498

by the 'snap-matchlock', operated by means of an internal spring action causing the cock, or serpentine, to snap forwards into the pan when pressure was applied to the trigger. By the 1550s, the snap-matchlock was itself superceded by a simpler sear-lock that relied on a long lever connected to an oscillating bar within the lock. Working against the action of a light mainspring, squeezing the trigger lever lowered the serpentine into the priming pan. Although this mechanism remained in use in Britain until the 1630s, from about 1600 an improved form known as the trigger, or 'tricker', lock was increasingly popular. Here, the lever was replaced by a separate trigger, of a more recognisably modern form, which was operated by the musketeer's index finger. This mechanism had a number of advantages over the older style, including the ability to fit a trigger-guard which greatly reduced the risk of accidental discharge.

Although relatively cheap, easy to produce and mechanically reliable, there were a number of disadvantages to the matchlock musket. In 1627

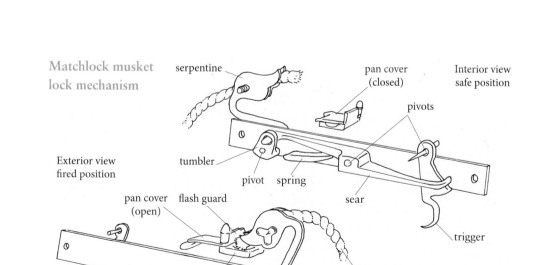

Matchlock musket
lock mechanism

serpentine

pan cover
(closed)

Interior view
safe position

pivots

Exterior view
fired position

tumbler

pivot   spring

sear

pan cover   flash guard
(open)

trigger

match-cord

lock plate   priming pan

Thomas Kellie remarked that he had seen many misfires due to a bad match, a poorly cocked match, wet weather and bad powder. Additionally, carrying a smouldering match cord around gunpowder had the potential to be extremely dangerous. At Edgehill in 1642 a soldier 'clapped his hand carelessly into a barrel of powder with his match between his fingers, whereby much powder was blown up and many killed'. At night the glow of a match cord could betray a soldier's position, though equally it could be used to mislead an enemy. (Following their victory at the battle of Sourton Down in 1643, the Parliamentarians hung lighted match cords in gorse bushes to deceive the Royalists whilst they withdrew.) Supplying sufficient quantities of match cords was often problematic. The garrison of Lyme, for example, which numbered 1500 men, used 560 lb of match in only twenty-four hours. Such a high rate of consumption was in part due to the recommended practice of keeping both ends of the match cord alight in case one end was extinguished.

The flintlock was another significant type of lock mechanism in use during the Civil Wars. The earliest flintlocks, otherwise known as snaphances, or snaphaunces (a term derived from the Dutch 'snaphaan' – literally 'snapping hen'), probably developed in Germany during the 1530s. The term 'snaphance' technically refers to all lock mechanisms operating on the flint-and-steel principle, though today it is more commonly associated

▲ Detail of a snaphance lockplate with a separate pan cover and steel, *c.*1645. Note the addition of the dog catch which provided additional safety to the half-cocked or safe position. XII.5392

with the earliest form with the steel and pan-cover made separately. Confusingly the contemporary word 'firelock' was used indiscriminately to refer to any type of firearm with either a flintlock or wheellock mechanism. The snaphance mechanism utilised a heavy V-shaped mainspring, which was compressed when the cock was drawn back. At full cock a smaller spring pushed a lug on the sear lever sideways through an aperture in the lockplate and engaged a projection on the tail of the cock, holding it and the compressed spring in place. When the trigger was pulled, the sear was released and the compressed spring caused the cock to swing forward and strike a piece of hardened steel mounted on a pivoting arm. At the same time the pan cover was opened by means of an internal pushrod attached to the tumbler. The impact of the flint pushed the steel out of the way, simultaneously producing a shower of sparks that fell onto the gunpowder in the priming pan. The forward motion of the cock was arrested by a small metal buffer fixed to the outside of the lockplate.

In England around the first quarter of the 17th century a significant improvement was made to the design of the snaphance mechanism, with the steel and pan-cover being combined into one simple L-shaped component. Known today as the 'English lock', this simpler and cheaper design meant that when the flint hit the steel, sparks were struck and the pan-cover was automatically thrown open in the same motion. Unlike the swivelling

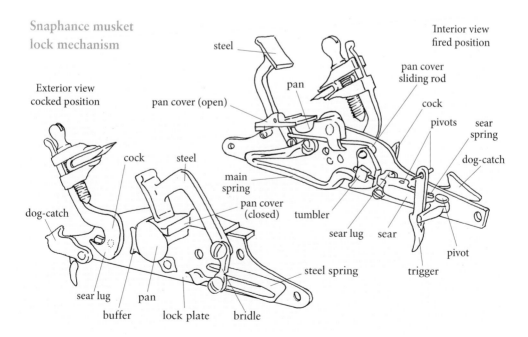

Snaphance musket lock mechanism

Interior view fired position

Exterior view cocked position

steel

pan

pan cover sliding rod

pan cover (open)

cock

pivots

sear spring

cock

steel

dog-catch

main spring

dog-catch

pan cover (closed)

tumbler

sear lug

sear

pivot

sear lug

pan

steel spring

trigger

buffer

lock plate

bridle

pan-covers found on matchlocks which were prone to damage, the combined steel and pan-cover provided the priming powder with relatively good protection from the elements. However, this development necessitated the addition of a safety device. On snaphances the firearm could be made safe simply by pushing the separate steel forward out of the way of the cock, all the time keeping the pan cover closed and the device cocked. Now that both elements were combined, this could not be done safely without the risk of accidental discharge. The problem was solved, on some but not all locks, with the addition to the lockplate of a small pivoted 'dog-catch' located at the rear of the cock which provided additional safety to the half-cock component of the lock's sear mechanism. This feature appears on locks of many designs and has given rise to the rather vague and non-specific term 'doglock' which neither indicates the type of lock mechanism or the country of origin. A number of older snaphances were converted to incorporate the

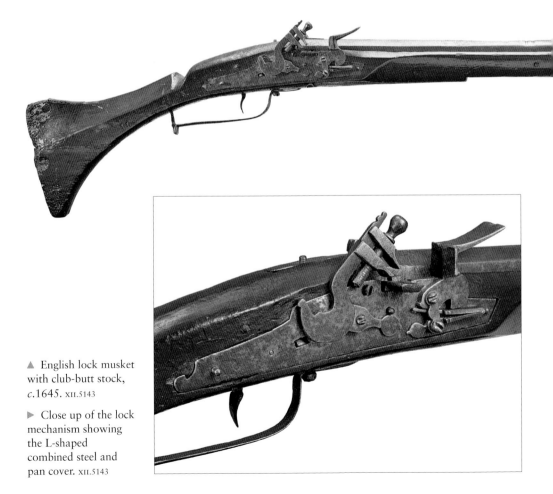

▲ English lock musket with club-butt stock, *c.*1645. XII.5143

▶ Close up of the lock mechanism showing the L-shaped combined steel and pan cover. XII.5143

combined L-shaped pan cover and steel whilst retaining their internal two-part sear mechanism. Although outwardly similar to the snaphance, the new English locks incorporated a variety of simpler but still horizontally-operating sears. Most lock mechanisms included a half-cock position, but this was still sometimes supplemented with a dog catch, especially on firearms where an additional safety measure was thought advisable.

Early in the 17th century, the French also developed a lock mechanism featuring a combined steel and pan-cover. However, in contrast to the English lock, the 'French lock' incorporated a vertically-operating sear and tumbler mechanism with a secure half-cock feature. Although this removed the need for a dog catch, some were nonetheless still fitted with them. By the late 1630s the sear mechanism found on 'French' locks had become almost universal throughout Europe and was found on almost all foreign firearms imported during the Civil Wars.

English lock musket
lock mechanism

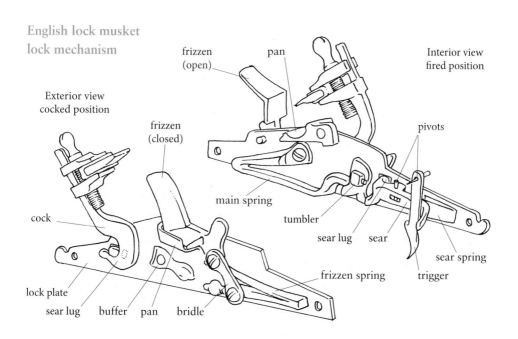

frizzen (open)

pan

Interior view
fired position

Exterior view
cocked position

frizzen (closed)

pivots

cock

main spring

tumbler

sear lug   sear

sear spring

lock plate

sear lug   buffer   pan   bridle

frizzen spring   trigger

The flintlock possessed many advantages over the matchlock. According to the Earl of Orrery, 'for the firelock you only have to cock, and you are prepared to shoot, but with your matchlock you have several motions, the least of which is as long a performing as but that one of the other'. Furthermore, as Richard Elton observed, there was no danger of a smouldering match coming into contact with loose gunpowder. Flintlocks were therefore ideal weapons to be issued to specialist companies such as those who guarded artillery trains. The Earl of Essex, for instance, had 400 'firelocks' under his general of ordnance, Lieutenant General Philibert Emmanual de Boyes, whilst Captain William Legge's firelocks guarded the Royalist artillery at the battle of Edgehill. The irregular nature of warfare in Ireland, combined with an unforgiving environment, certainly made the flintlock a useful weapon. Apart from 400 firelocks serving in the Lord Lieutenant's Regiment, there were numerous other independent English companies, such as those under Captains Francis Langley and Thomas Sandford.

Nonetheless, the matchlock remained the most common infantry firearm principally due to its lower cost as well as being more robust and easier to maintain. In 1645, for example, the cost of a matchlock musket was between 10s 0d to 11s 6d compared to 14s 4d to 15s 6d for a flintlock. During the course of the Civil Wars the proportion of flintlocks to matchlocks gradually increased. According to the contracts of supply for the New Model Army, in 1645 the ratio of snaphances to matchlocks was roughly 1:5 or 1:6; by 1650 this had increased to between 1:3 and 1:4. On 13 February 1649/50, for example, the Council of State ordered 300 flintlock/snaphance and 1000 matchlock muskets from the London gunmakers Christopher Fell and Edward Burrows for a total cost of £1,304 3s 4d.

The weight of the musket made it a cumbersome weapon to use in the field, and required the use of a forked rest. This comprised a wooden staff with a U-shaped metal bracket at the top and a spike at the bottom in order to prevent it slipping during firing. Musket rests were still being issued during the early years of the war: in 1643 Colonel Langham's Parliamentarian regiment received 711 muskets and 703 rests, whilst the following year the Royalists received 1500 muskets with rests, scourers, bandoliers and bullet-moulds from the Low Countries. However, by this date musket rests were falling out of use thanks to the introduction of a lighter musket. Indeed, the London gunmaker William Watson stopped supplying musket rests after 1642 and there are no references to them among the 1645 contracts of supply for the New Model Army. In 1630 the Council of War's 'Order for the general uniformitie of all sortes of armes both for horse and foote' specified that muskets should be 62 inches in length, with a barrel of 48 inches and a bore of 12 bullets for every pound of lead – in other words, '12 bore'. This was reiterated in the 1639 'Directions for Musters'. The following year the Ordnance officers recommended the adoption of a lighter musket with 3½-foot barrels.

◄ A mid-17th century musket rest. The quality of the metal heads varied considerably. XIII.917

▼ Musketeer's equipment including a musket rest as depicted in Henry Hexham's *Principles of the Art Military* (1637).

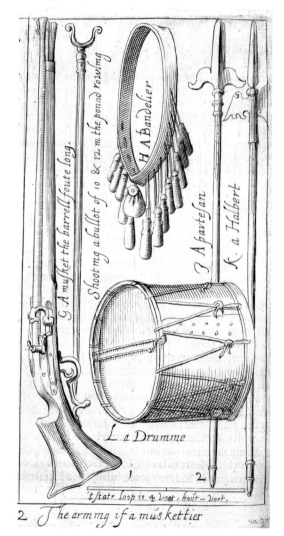

As a result the Council of War placed an order for 5,000 muskets with 4½-foot barrels weighing 14 lb and 10,000 with the reduced 3½-foot barrels weighing 12 lb. Despite the efforts at standardisation, issues of supply, particularly from abroad, meant that reality was often quite different. The Royalist captain John Strachan lamented: 'and the muskets, there are about 1000 of them, I am assured they are of 3, or 5 score sundry bores, some pistol bores, some carbine bores, some little fowling peeces, and all the old trash that could be rapt together'. Such a mixture of bores resulted in men biting or cutting off pieces of lead from their bullets in order to make them fit. Indeed, uniformity as such was not fully achieved until the introduction of 'pattern' firearms in the 1730s.

Matchlocks featured priming pans and flash-guards which were fitted separately, whereas on flintlocks the priming pan was made integral with the lock. It was not uncommon for matchlock barrels to be re-used on flintlocks, though in order to accommodate the different mechanism the priming pan and flash-guard was removed and the recesses filled in. The usual method of attaching the barrel to the stock was via a vertical screw through the breech-tang, together with pins which passed through small pierced lugs on the underside of the barrel. Musket stocks were usually made from walnut, pear or beech, although as Gervase Markham noted they could be made from any 'fast, firm and smoothe light wood'. The two most common forms were the so-called 'fish-tailed' and 'club' butts. The former developed at the end of the 16th century and was characterised by its splayed butt, with concave sides forming a truncated triangle. Although elegant, the comb of the fish-tail butt was vulnerable to damage. As such many were provided with a metal butt plate sometimes with the addition of a narrow metal strap running along the comb. In contrast, the more rounded and sturdy club-butt, which appeared in the 1620s, was not only more robust but was also more comfortable to use. As a result it had superseded the fish-tail butt by the 1660s. Apart from its obvious value as a firearm, the weight and shape of the musket's stock made it an effective club for close-quarter fighting. At the battle of Naseby in 1645 the Earl of Clarendon related how the king's infantry fired a single volley before 'falling in with their swords and butt ends of muskets; with which they did very notable execution'.

By the beginning of the 17th century ammunition was usually carried in a bandolier rather than a powder-flask. Invented in the first half of the 16th century, the bandolier comprised a leather belt from which were suspended at least twelve bottles known as charges or 'boxes', each containing enough gunpowder for a single shot. Many also included a small pouch for lead bullets and a flask to hold the priming powder. A number of bandolier belts

► Collar of bandoliers
with priming bottle,
bullet pouch and
shoulder pad. The blue
and white strings are
restored. XIII.354

incorporated a pad of leather or felt at the shoulder in order to lessen the
discomfort of shouldering a heavy musket. Typically costing between 14*d*
and *20d* each, those listed in the contracts for the New Model Army in 1645
were 'boxes of wood with whole bottoms to be turned within and not
boared [in order to hold more powder] the heads to be of wood & to be layd
in oyle vizt three tymes over & to be coloured blue with blewe and white
strings of strong thread twist &wth good belts at xxd a peece'. The problem
with using wooden bottles was the tendency for the wood to swell if it
became wet, making the top difficult to remove. As a simple weather-
proofing measure, the bottles were sometimes covered with leather or a
spark-resistant metal such as pewter, tin, copper or tinned iron.

During the early stages of the war the Royalist musketeers of the Oxford Army were forced to carry their gunpowder either in their pockets or in leather powder bags made by the city's glovers and bookbinders. Between June and October 1643 an estimated 1,081 powder bags were issued to the Royalists. Rather than simply carrying the powder loose in the bag, which would have been highly hazardous and difficult to use, the gunpowder was probably contained in cartridges. These consisted of a tube of white paper which contained a measure of gunpowder for one shot and a lead bullet. To load the firearm, the bullet was bitten off and the gunpowder poured down the barrel, after which the bullet was rammed down.

Although convenient, bandoliers could also be hazardous. According to the Earl of Orrery, 'I have often seen much prejudice in the use of bandoleers, which being worn in the belts for them above the soldiers' coats, are often apt to take fire, especially if the matchlock musket be used; and when they take fire, they commonly wound and often kill him that wears that, and those near him'.

In addition to the bandolier or powder bag, a musketeer would also have been equipped with a brush and screw to fix to one end of the ramrod to clean the barrel and extract the bullet in case of a misfire. A priming pin was also used to clear residue from the touch hole which if left would prevent sparks from the priming pan reaching the main charge – in other words, causing 'a flash in the pan'.

It was generally agreed by contemporary military theorists that it was best to withhold musket fire until the enemy were close in order to avoid wasting powder and shot. At the battle of Kilsyth in August 1645 the commander of the Scottish Parliamentarians, William Ballie, recounted how his musketeers 'made more fire than I could have wished; and therefore I did what I could ... to make them spare their shott till the enemy should be at a nearer distance'. According to the Elizabethan soldier John Smythe, whilst acknowledging that a musket ball could be carried up to 600 yards, recommended withholding fire until the enemy

▶ A mid-17th century musketeer's priming flask with original velvet covering. XIII.230

were within eight, ten or twelve paces. By the time of the Civil Wars, effective distance was considered to be within 100 yards with some commanders waiting until the enemy were only 10 yards distance.

In addition to conventional muskets, some men were issued with 'birding' or 'fowling' guns to act as snipers. General Monck, for instance, recommended that six men in each company should be equipped as snipers in order to pick off enemy officers and harry the flanks of an opposing force. At Bradford in 1642 the Royalist master-gunner was killed by a Parliamentarian sniper, whilst at Sherborne in 1645 two former park-keepers with long fowling-pieces were employed by the Royalists. In 1652, 500 fowling-pieces with five-foot barrels were ordered by Parliament for service in Scotland.

▲ Illustration (No. 43) of the musketeer's drill from *Wappenhandelinghe* by Jacob de Gheyn (1607).

PISTOLS AND CARBINES

In addition to a sword and perhaps a short pollaxe, the cavalry of the Civil Wars were frequently armed with a pair of pistols or a carbine. Although the majority of infantry firearms were matchlocks, the mechanism required both hands to operate and was thus impractical for use on horseback. Consequently, cavalry firearms were fitted either with wheel- or flintlock mechanisms. The development of the wheellock mechanism was a momentous step since it allowed – for the first time – the reliable use of firearms from horseback. This had a significant impact on the development of cavalry tactics.

Invented early in the 16th century, the wheellock operated on a similar principle to a modern cigarette lighter: sparks were generated by a grooved steel wheel revolving against a piece of iron pyrites'. Power was provided by a heavy V-shaped mainspring attached to the wheel by a short length of transmission chain. Once the barrel had been loaded, a key or spanner was

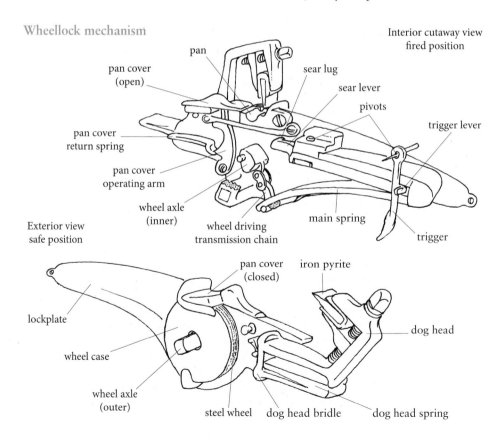

Wheellock mechanism

Interior cutaway view
fired position

pan

pan cover
(open)

sear lug

sear lever

pivots

trigger lever

pan cover
return spring

pan cover
operating arm

wheel axle
(inner)

Exterior view
safe position

wheel driving
transmission chain

main spring

trigger

pan cover
(closed)

iron pyrite

lockplate

wheel case

dog head

wheel axle
(outer)

steel wheel   dog head bridle

dog head spring

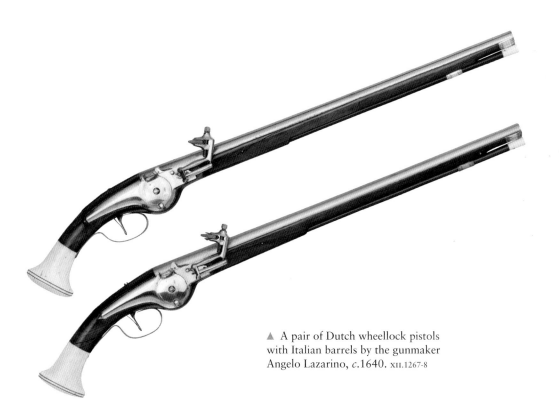

▲ A pair of Dutch wheellock pistols
with Italian barrels by the gunmaker
Angelo Lazarino, *c.*1640. XII.1267-8

used to turn the wheel clockwise for about three-quarters of a turn, causing
the chain to wrap around its spindle and compressing the mainspring.
The wheel was then held in position by a rounded lug on the end of a
horizontally acting sear which passed through an aperture in the lockplate
and was pressed by a spring into a recess on its inner surface which locked it
in place. The pan was filled with priming powder and the pan cover closed.
The wheellock could then be left in this position until it was needed. Prior to
pulling the trigger, the dog holding the pyrites was manually lowered to rest
upon the pan cover. When the trigger was pulled and the wheel began to
revolve, the pan cover was automatically thrown open, allowing the pyrites to
make contact with the edge of the wheel. The sparks created would ignite the
priming powder. In 1644 John Vernon recommended 'if thou beest furnished
with one Carbine and two Pistols, fire thy Carbine, and one of thy Pistols at
thine Enemies, but always reserve one of thy Pistols readie charged, primed,
spand and cocked in thy houlster'. This practice though, was not without its
disadvantages as a number of contemporary writers noted that wheellocks
were prone to jamming if left spanned for too long. The wheellock mechanism
changed very little during the first half of the 17th century, although there was
a tendency towards simplifying it and making it more compact.

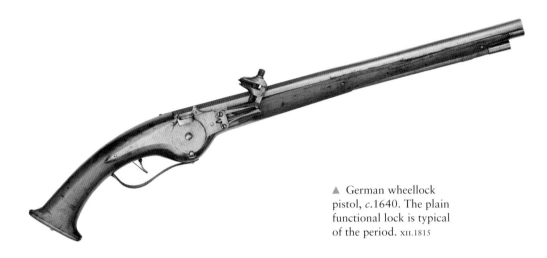

▲ German wheellock pistol, *c.*1640. The plain functional lock is typical of the period. XII.1815

Due to their complex mechanisms, wheellocks required very high standards of manufacture. As such it remained an expensive weapon, issued only in small numbers: in 1631, for example, the rates of pay for gunmakers specified £3 for a pair of wheellocks, compared to £2 for a pair of flintlocks. In 1640, sixteen London gunmakers supplied 'Pistolles with Fiere Lockes fournished with holsters, worm scorer mould and keyes per pece' at £2 16*s* 0*d*. Prince Rupert appears to have equipped at least some of his troop of horse with wheellocks, writing as he did in October 1642 to Sir John Heydon, Lieutenant General of the King's Ordnance, for '30tie paire of your best holster and as many of your best spanners and as many of your best flaskes'.

The vast majority of wheellocks were produced on the Continent, particularly Germany and the Netherlands. Indeed, relatively few wheellocks were produced in England and there is no evidence for their manufacture in Scotland or Ireland. Consequently, with their reliance on foreign imports the Royalists appear to have made greater use of them, although they were nonetheless still imported by Parliament.

In the 16th and early 17th centuries many pistols featured long barrels, making them heavy and awkward to use. Consequently from the 1620s there was a general reduction in barrel length to make the firearms lighter and more manageable. In 1630 the Council of War decreed that pistols should be 26 inches long, with a barrel of 18 inches and a bore of 24 bullets to the pound. In 1639 Ordnance Officers experimented with barrel length and found that a pistol barrel of 16 inches was just as accurate as one of 18 inches. Although 18-inch barrels were retained as standard, many Civil War pistols were produced with barrels of only 14 to 16 inches, yet with no discernible loss of accuracy.

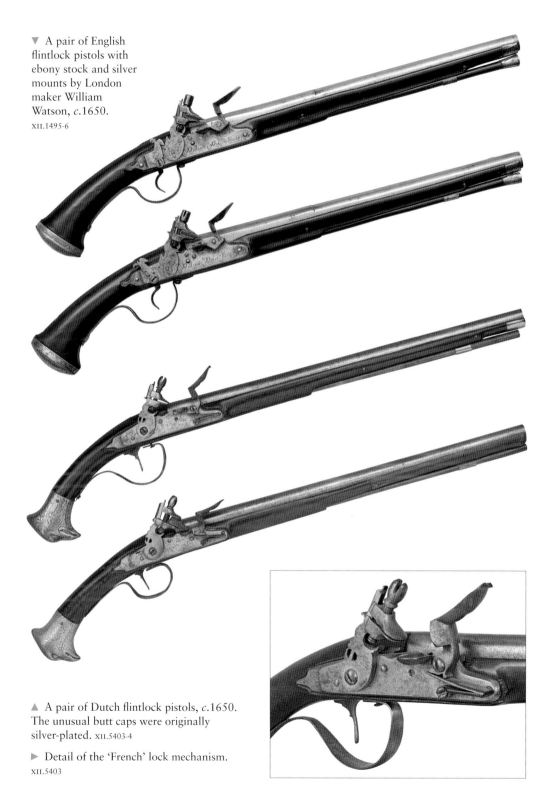

▼ A pair of English flintlock pistols with ebony stock and silver mounts by London maker William Watson, *c.*1650. XII.1495-6

▲ A pair of Dutch flintlock pistols, *c.*1650. The unusual butt caps were originally silver-plated. XII.5403-4

▶ Detail of the 'French' lock mechanism. XII.5403

▲ English flintlock pistol by Robert Murden
of London, c.1645. XII.5414

▶ Detail of the lockplate, showing the
maker's name flanked by fleur-de-lys. XII.5414

In general pistol stocks of the period were much more slender than they
had been in the preceding century, with an emphasis towards simplicity of
line rather than complex decoration. Decoration though was not entirely
absent. On a number of pistols, such as those by the noted London
gunmaker Robert Murden, delicate leaf-forms were carved around the barrel
tang and finial of the trigger guard. One of the main developments in the
early 1600s was a change to the shape of the pistol butt, which from around
1620 was simply cut off straight and fitted with a metal cap. A number of
high-quality pistols were fitted with ebony stocks and silver butt-caps. From
the 1630s some Continental pistols incorporated ivory, metal or ebony
pommels in the form of human or animal heads.

One interesting type of stock found on flintlock pistols was the bellied, or
wheellock, form that appeared in Britain around 1640. Whilst it is possible
that this form was the result of wheellock stocks and lockplates being reused
on flintlocks, wheellocks were never produced in such large numbers that
would have created a surplus of parts. Instead, the bellied stock and
lockplate appears to have been introduced into Britain by Dutch gunmakers
working in London, as well as via high-quality imports. Indeed, lists of
licensed exports in the National Archives at The Hague indicate that
Amsterdam alone exported over 29,000 pairs of pistols to England between
1639 and 1645. Consequently, many English-made pistols incorporated this
fashionable design.

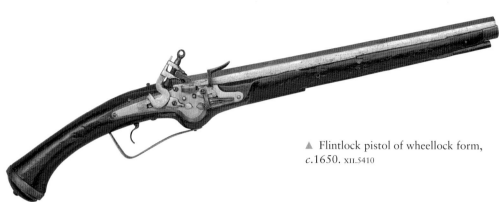

▲ Flintlock pistol of wheellock form,
*c.*1650. XII.5410

Two main types of stock were found on Scottish pistols during the first half of the 17th century: the fish-tail butt and the lemon, or globose, butt. From the late 1640s the heart-shaped butt became increasingly popular. Unlike elsewhere in Britain, the majority of Scottish pistols were fitted with lightweight metal stocks either of iron or brass, though some were made with walnut or Brazilwood with metal mounts. This preference for metal stocks can be explained by the fact that many Scottish gunmakers came from metal-working backgrounds, belonging to the guilds of Hammermen found in various towns.

The barrels on Scottish pistols were usually made of the same metal as the stock, although those with wooden stocks were provided with either brass or iron barrels. During the 17th century most fish-tail pistols were made of brass, whereas those with lemon-butts were generally of brass and steel. It should be noted that these were not the firearms of ordinary cavalrymen, but the preserve of wealthier individuals. Instead, with the largely Edinburgh-based industry too small to meet demand, the vast majority of munition-quality pieces had to be imported. Between 22 August 1642 and 19 April 1644, Scotland imported 26,140 pairs of pistols and around 60,000 muskets from Antwerp alone.

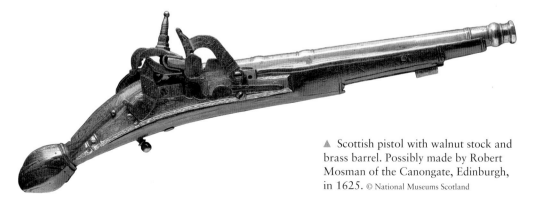

▲ Scottish pistol with walnut stock and brass barrel. Possibly made by Robert Mosman of the Canongate, Edinburgh, in 1625. © National Museums Scotland

Some cavalrymen were also equipped with carbines. In 1635 William Barriffe remarked that harquebusiers carried 'a Case of Pistols, short, and a Carbine (hanging by in a Belt and Swivel on his Right side)'. The carbine, which had been developed in the 16th century, was a short, relatively light gun designed for mounted use. In 1630 the English Council of War specified that the carbine or 'petronel' was to be 45 inches long with a barrel of 30 inches and a bore of 24 balls to the pound. However, as with all firearms there was no standardisation, particularly when it came to foreign imports. By the 17th century the harquebus, after which mounted harquebusiers were named, was very similar to the carbine aside from having a larger bore. From the 1620s, however, the harquebus began to fall out of use and by the 1630s it had been largely replaced with the carbine (although, confusingly, both terms were largely interchangeable by this date).

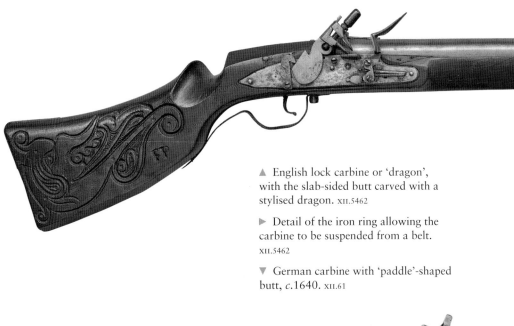

▲ English lock carbine or 'dragon', with the slab-sided butt carved with a stylised dragon. XII.5462

▶ Detail of the iron ring allowing the carbine to be suspended from a belt. XII.5462

▼ German carbine with 'paddle'-shaped butt, c.1640. XII.61

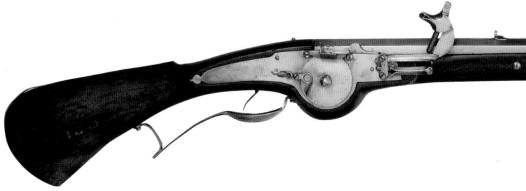

Another type of firearm closely related to the carbine was the 'Dragon'. According to Gervase Markham these were 'short peeces of 16 inches the Barrell, and full Musquet bore, with firelocks'. It is worth noting, though, that the name 'Dragon' may have been applied to any short-barrelled, large-bore cavalry firearm which was later replaced by the term 'blunderbuss'. In January 1645 a contract was placed for 'two hundred snaphance Dragoones full bore & proofe' at 12s 4d each. Although by the time of the Civil Wars dragoons were primarily armed with muskets, it is possible these soldiers were originally named after this type of firearm. Essentially mounted infantry, dragoons arrived on the battlefield on horseback but dismounted to fight.

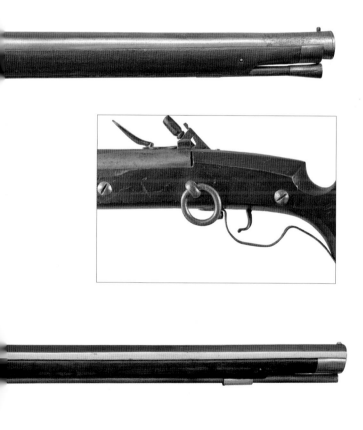

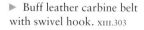

▶ Buff leather carbine belt with swivel hook. XIII.303

▲ Portrait of a Dutch officer holding a wheellock carbine attached to his belt by means of a bar and sliding ring, 1624. © Mauritshuis, The Hague

In 1639 the price of a wheellock carbine was recorded as £1 16*s* compared to £1 2*s* for a flintlock. During the war prices varied depending on where the carbines were being purchased. For example, Parliament was purchasing carbines from London gunmakers for 12*s* 9*d* each, whereas the Royalists were paying £1 11*s* (that is, considerably more than double) for those imported from the Netherlands. Parliament does not appear to have made such widespread use of the carbine as the Royalists, however, this situation seems to have changed after 1649. On 27 February 1650/1, for example, four London gunmakers were paid £350 for 600 carbines and swivels (belts) for the war in Ireland.

Although bandoliers were widely used by the infantry, the cavalry predominantly used powder flasks or cartridges, due to their practicality on horseback. Horn powder flasks were made by boiling cows' horns in water until soft, and then moulding into the desired shape. A wooden base was inserted at the bottom and the nozzle, made from pewter, iron or brass, was fitted to the top. Powder flasks were also constructed of wood and sometimes covered with leather or textile. The Earl of Orrery recommended that cartridge bottles should be of tin 'because they are not so oft to break as Wooden ones are, and do not in wet Weather or lying in the Tents, relax'.

With a longer barrel and larger bore, the carbine had an advantage over the pistol in both range and power. As such, it was usually discharged prior to coming in close contact with the enemy. At the battle of Roundway Down, the Royalist Sir John Byron recorded that the orders were given that 'Not a man should discharge his pistol till the enemy had spent all his shot, which was punctually observed, so that first they gave us a volley of their carbines, then of their pistols, then we fell with them'. John Vernon also recommended that carbines were to be fired 'at a convenient distance' before engaging with pistols. Pistols were really only effective at close range, especially when facing armoured opponents. Indeed, it was not uncommon to wait until the enemy was within arm's length before firing. The Parliamentarian colonel John Birch, for instance, recorded that he came so close to his adversary that 'my pistoll touched his side; where I shott him, his scarf was fired with the powder, and downe hee fell'. At any great distance, pistol fire had little effect: at the battle of Megray Hill (1639) it was noted that 'Many pistoll shott wer exchanged, but at too great distaunce on both sydes most shottes; otherwayes the continuall motione of ther horses preveened all hurt'. Indeed, at Marston Moor (1644) Edmund Ludlow reported that 'the horse on both sides behaved themselves with the utmost bravery; for having discharged their pistols, and flung them at each others heads, they fell to it with their swords'.

SWORDS

Whilst swords had been made in Britain since the early Middle Ages, they were not produced in sufficient quantity to equip large armies. As such, prior to the Civil Wars many swords and separate blades had to be imported from the Continent. The main source of European blades was Solingen in western Germany, which had a long history of metal-working. However, the outbreak of the Thirty Years War witnessed the collapse of the city's sword-making industry which took a number of years to recover. As a result many bladesmiths took up residence in the Low Countries. In 1629 a number of these men were recruited by Sir John Heydon, the king's Lieutenant of Ordnance, to establish a sword-making 'manufactury' in England. A mill for grinding and polishing blades was set up on Hounslow Heath in 1630 and leased by the London Cutler Benjamin Stone, and from 1636 Stone received contracts to supply large numbers of swords. By the time of the Bishops' Wars (1639) Hounslow had become a vital industry. Nonetheless, in order to fulfil large contracts, blades were also brought in from London, Birmingham and the Continent. Following the departure of many of the Hounslow swordsmiths to Oxford at the outbreak of war in 1642, a number of the mills came under the control of Parliament and were converted for the production of gunpowder. Nonetheless, swords continued to be produced at Hounslow with the Parliamentarian commander Sir William Waller ordering '200 horsemen's swords' in April 1643.

Parliament also relied on the sword makers of London, particularly the Worshipful Company of Cutlers who received their Royal Charter in 1416. Lacking the ability to produce large numbers of blades in London the Cutlers obtained their blades from various wholesalers before 'working' them into swords by making hilts and scabbards. They were contracted by the Office of Ordnance to supply the New Model Army with significant quantities of swords. On 11 July 1645, a contract was placed for '2000 swords and Belts Dutch blades at 4s 6d a piece'. One estimate suggests that London arms makers produced roughly 102,000 swords between 1642 and 1651.

◀ Robert Rich, 2nd earl of Warwick and Parliament's Lord High Admiral, wearing what appears to be an elaborate English rapier. © National Maritime Museum

Following the move to Oxford, the Royalists initially relied on local swordsmiths to provide them with weapons. However, on 20 June 1643 the Council of War instructed grindstones and wheels to be fitted to the cannon-boring equipment in Christ Church College in order to grind sword blades. Later that same year a mill was built at Woolvercroft near Oxford for the production of swords, whilst the main forge was located in the city at Gloucester Hall.

Throughout the wars, the various combatants relied heavily on foreign imports. In 1639 the English merchant adventurer John Quarles, living in Rotterdam, exported 12,323 swords, 10,859 sword belts and 1,650 girdles for delivery to the king's forces, whilst in 1643 the Antwerp merchant Daniel Fourment exported 3,000 swords amongst other equipment to the Royalists

▶ English mortuary-hilt sword with a German blade made in Solingen ('IHN SOLINGEN'). IX.1086

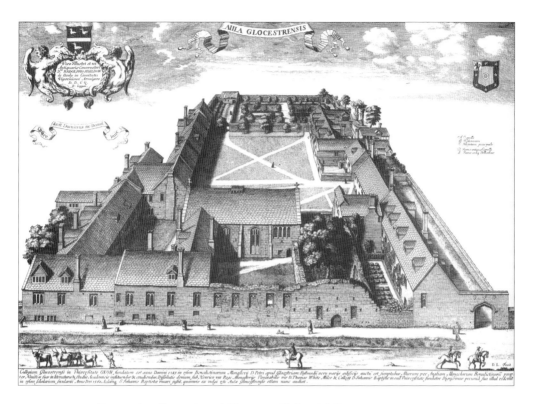

▲ Copperplate illustration of Gloucester Hall, *c*.1675. Private collection.

in Newcastle. Compared with England, however, Scottish sword production was on a much more modest scale. It involved a variety of armourers, guardmakers, cutlers and lorimers based in towns such as Edinburgh, Glasgow, Stirling and Aberdeen. As with England the majority of blades were imported from the Continent before being fitted with Scottish-made hilts. Many blades came from Germany, with those bearing the forged name of the 16th-century north Italian swordsmith Andrea Ferrara being particularly popular.

At the outbreak of the war a considerable amount of effort was expended cleaning and repairing swords which had been donated, seized or obtained from the various county militia stores. Swords were certainly not always in plentiful supply. At the battle of Tippermuir (1644) the Earl of Montrose's men had neither pikes nor swords, and had to resort to throwing stones when attacked by cavalry. Indeed, the Earl of Orrery lamented that 'it is both a grief, and a shame, to see how few Pikemen, in most of our ordinary Companies, have Swords by their sides, and the Musketeers seldom any'. The quality of ordinary munition swords appears to have been variable as according to Sir James Turner they were 'for the most part extremely base'.

Essentially a sword with a long, narrow, symmetrical two-edged blade primarily designed for thrusting, the rapier was as much a status symbol and fashion accessory as a practical fighting weapon. Largely confined to officers and wealthy individuals, the distinction between a rapier intended for war and one intended for civilian use is somewhat blurred. However, although opinion was divided, at the time rapiers were generally considered unsuitable for use on the battlefield. The 1615 play 'Worke for Cutlers: or, a merry Dialogue betweene Sword, Rapier and Dagger' included the notable following lines: 'Rapier a Soulder? When did you ere know Rapier to fight a Batell … No, no, its Sworde that's a notable Souldier'. Nonetheless, a Parliamentarian report of the battle of Chalgrove Field (1643) noted that the 'Cavaleirs having long Rapiers and Swords, a foot and a halfe longer than ordinary, did herewith much annoy the Parliament Forces'. In 1642 the Lord Justices in Dublin wrote to the House of Commons for 4,000 basket-hilted swords and 4,000 rapiers. It is possible that in these instances reference was being made to what are sometimes known as 'Riding Swords'; characterised by a rapier style hilt but a broader and more robust blade which was suitable for both thrusting and cutting.

Many rapiers were richly decorated with striking designs in gold and silver, reflecting the taste and status of the owner. As French fencing author François Dancie noted in 1623, the rapier was 'the finest plume of a great man'. Other designs, more practical for the field, incorporated steel hilts with restrained pierced and chiselled decoration. In England one popular form featured a pierced cup and tightly-wound quillons which scrolled towards the blade; another incorporated two or three circular guards atop a pierced cup, linked by a number of short bars. On the Continent a style of hilt known today as a 'Pappenheimer' became fashionable from the 1620s. Depicted in numerous Dutch portraits of the 1630s and 1640s, the hilt – which was also fitted to other styles of sword blades – incorporated large pierced plates and long recurved quillons.

▶ German or English rapier hilt with German blade, *c*.1630. The hilt has been decorated with fleur-de-lys and Prince of Wales feathers. IX.956

◄ English rapier, c.1620, with pierced cup surmounted by circular guards. ɪx.1380

▼ Detail of the inscription: 'FOR MY CHRIST RESOLVED TO DY/WHO I [?]AVES ME LET HIM WARE ME'. ɪx.1380

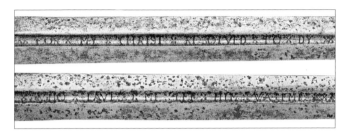

► An example of a Pappenheimer hilt with pierced plates and recurved quillons, c.1635. ɪx.5628

▼ High-quality rapier with English hilt and Italian blade, c.1620-30. ɪx.883

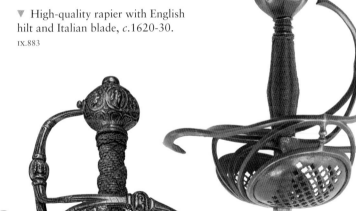

HANGERS

During the 17th century, the term 'hanger' was interchangeable with 'cutlass' and referred to any short sword, usually with a curved blade, which could be comfortably worn when fighting on foot. Hangers were equally popular as civilian and hunting weapons. It is possible that the 'tuck' (from the French *estoc*, 'to thrust') was also related to the hanger, particularly the short variety General Monck recommended for musketeers and pikemen. The term 'tuck', presumably referring to the longer type used from horseback, was also confusingly synonymous with 'rapier'.

Characteristic features of English-made hangers of the 1640s included a mushroom-cap pommel, a large tang button and baluster decoration to the knucklebow which was frequently echoed on the quillon terminal. Many hilts incorporated two shell-shaped guards – the outer one larger and curved towards the point, the inner one smaller and curved in the opposite direction towards the pommel – whereas others had hilts with equal-sized guards both curving towards the pommel.

▶ English hanger with an imported German blade, *c*.1640 IX.2783

▶ Detail of the hilt showing the chiselled decoration. IX.2783

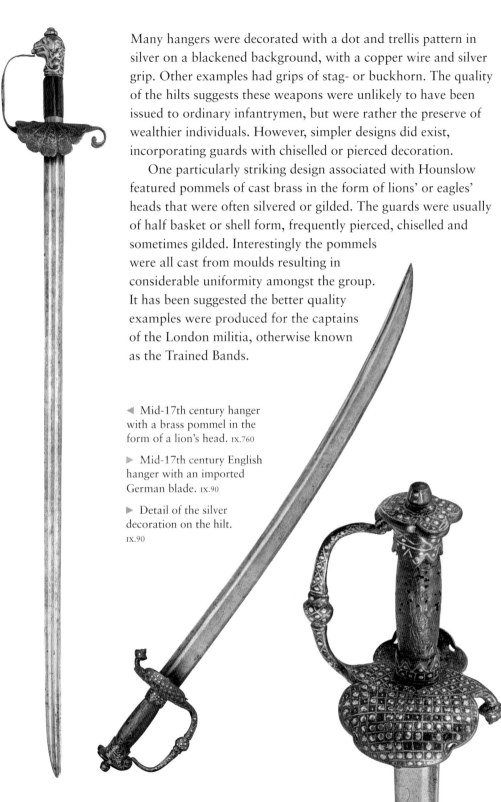

Many hangers were decorated with a dot and trellis pattern in silver on a blackened background, with a copper wire and silver grip. Other examples had grips of stag- or buckhorn. The quality of the hilts suggests these weapons were unlikely to have been issued to ordinary infantrymen, but were rather the preserve of wealthier individuals. However, simpler designs did exist, incorporating guards with chiselled or pierced decoration.

One particularly striking design associated with Hounslow featured pommels of cast brass in the form of lions' or eagles' heads that were often silvered or gilded. The guards were usually of half basket or shell form, frequently pierced, chiselled and sometimes gilded. Interestingly the pommels were all cast from moulds resulting in considerable uniformity amongst the group. It has been suggested the better quality examples were produced for the captains of the London militia, otherwise known as the Trained Bands.

◀ Mid-17th century hanger with a brass pommel in the form of a lion's head. IX.760

▶ Mid-17th century English hanger with an imported German blade. IX.90

▶ Detail of the silver decoration on the hilt. IX.90

BASKET HILTS

The basket hilt was developed in the early 16th century to provide better protection for an unarmoured hand. By the time of the Civil Wars, it was a particular favourite of the cavalry. Basket hilts were fitted to both broadsword and backsword blades, the latter of which had only a single sharpened edge. Common in Britain, they were chiefly associated with Highland Scotland, and earned a mention in an early-17th century poem lampooning the Scots who accompanied James VI and I to England in 1603:

Bonny Scot all witness can,
England has made thee a gentleman …
The sword at thy haunch was a great black blade,
With a great basket-hilt of iron made
But now a long rapier doth hang by thy side,
And huffingly doth this bonny Scot ride.

At the time there was a tendency in England and Lowland Scotland to group together the inhabitants of Ireland and Highland Scotland under the name 'Irish', meaning 'Gaelic speaking'. As such the term 'Irish hilt' was used by the English to describe the basket hilt, whereas in Scotland it was usually referred to as a 'Highland Guard' or 'Highland Hilt'.

English references to swords with 'Irishe hiltes' first appeared in the early 17th century and their use continued throughout the Civil Wars. The last contract for Irish hilts appears to have

◄ Portrait of Colonel John Huchinson, governor of Nottingham Castle during the Civil Wars. He carries a fine gilt or copper-alloy 'Irish' basket hilt. © National Army Museum

been in 1653 when the English Committee for the Ordnance contracted 1,000 swords 'with stronge Irish Hilts and large for ye hand well ioyned over ye shoulder of ye blade'. The Irish hilt was formed of a guard of vertical bars that formed pointed arches or ovals. Space between the main framework was filled with shorter diagonal bars with a rectangular or round lozenge at the centre. Munition-grade Irish hilts were usually made from plain iron with decoration limited to simple incised lines. By contrast the finest examples were richly decorated with silver damascening on a blackened ground.

◀ Irish hilt broadsword with crude incised decoration, mid 17th century. ɪx.223

▶ A good quality Irish hilt broadsword, early 17th century. ɪx.1114

▼ Detail of the hilt showing the inlaid silver decoration in the form of tendrils and whorls. ɪx.1114

◀ A mortuary sword, the blade dated 1634 by IOHANNES HOPPIE of Greenwich. IX.1378

▼ A mid-17th century mortuary sword with a German blade. The hilt features an attractive 'feathered' decoration. IX.1022

▼ Hilt of a mortuary sword reputed to have been carried by Oliver Cromwell at the siege of Drogheda (1649). IX.1096

Unique to Britain, the so-called 'Mortuary sword' or 'Mortuary hilt' is probably the best known of all Civil War-era basket-hilted swords. The term 'Mortuary hilt' does not appear in any 17th-century sources, having been coined by 19th-century antiquarians and collectors in reference to the male faces found on many of the hilts. Many bear a likeness to Charles I, and it was thought these swords were produced in memory of the martyred king, although the fact that as they also appear on swords pre-dating the Civil Wars makes this unlikely. Instead, the majority of faces, some of which are female, most likely reflect the continuation of an Elizabethan tradition for depicting decorative masks on furniture and ornament. Nonetheless, a few hilts did incorporate crowned heads with the monogram 'CR' (*Carolus Rex*), though these were probably produced during the lifetime of the king and not afterwards.

The classic mortuary hilt incorporated a dish-shaped guard with a central knucklebow, and two side guards linked by one, two or three scrolled crossbars which were screwed into a fig-shaped pommel. The interior of the hilt would probably have been fitted with a leather lining. In place of a quillon, the guard plate was extended into a narrow scroll. The decoration on mortuary swords varied considerably. Apart from chiselled faces other designs featured delicate foliage and tendrils, riders on horseback, animal heads or petal-like patterns. Some lower-quality decorative schemes, some of which consisted of crudely chiselled faces and leaves, were produced in such large numbers that they have been considered regulation or 'pattern' swords. However, the term is somewhat anachronistic for this period as there is no evidence for a proscribed regulation design which, at least in theory, swordmakers had to copy. Indeed, it was not until 1796 that the first 'true' pattern swords came into service in the British army. As such, these earlier swords should be seen as being of 'munition type'.

Finally, the term 'proto-mortuary' has been applied to swords which have similar characteristics to the mortuary hilt but are generally of simpler design. Although these swords have consequently been considered to pre-date the 'fully developed' mortuary hilt, there is no firm evidence of this. Indeed, both styles appear to have been in use simultaneously. Proto-mortuary hilts were usually formed of two similarly sized shell-guards formed from a single plate of metal. Unlike the mortuary hilt, proto-mortuary hilts featured a fully developed quillon that extended from the shell-guards.

◀ A typical 'proto-mortuary' sword with shell-like guards. IX.1388

STAFF WEAPONS

PIKES

Extolled by contemporaries as 'the Queen of weapons', the pike was viewed as a noble weapon due to its long history stretching back to the days of Alexander the Great. Bearing one was seen as the mark of a gentleman; indeed, 'to trail a pike' was the contemporary phrase to describe a gentleman going off to war. Pikes occasionally appeared in portraits, where they clearly acted as badges of rank as well as serving as indicators of the subjects' martial prowess.

Although the 1639 'Directions for Musters' specified that pikes were to be 'seventeen foot long head and all', issues during the Civil Wars indicate there was very little standardisation. In part, this was caused by the multiple suppliers upon which each side was forced to rely. For example, in January 1642/3 15-foot pike staves were delivered into the king's stores at Oxford by the pike-maker Thomas Hill, whereas on 23 December 1645 John Thacker of London supplied the New Model Army with '400 pikes of good ash & sixteen foote long with steele heads at 3s 10d a peece'. To make matters worse, many men, even within the same regiment, took to shortening their pikes to make them more manageable. The consequences of one side having shorter pikes than the other could be disastrous. At the battle of Benburb in Ireland (1646), confederates under Owen Roe O'Neil were able to heavily defeat the Scottish Covenanters in part due to their longer pikes.

Pike staves were usually made of ash, or another lightweight wood, an inch and three-quarters in diameter. To improve their balance and make them easier to wield, many were tapered towards the head. As this considerably increased the risk of breakage (and to stop the heads being intentionally cut off), pikes were equipped with thin iron langets up to six foot long, which were nailed down the length of the shaft.

◀ Portrait of an unknown officer carrying a leading staff in the form of an elaborately pierced spear or pike-head, 1641. © The Knole Estate

▼ Illustration (No. 21) of the pikeman's drill from *Wappenhandelinghe* by Jacob de Gheyn (1607).

▶ A 16th-century Italian pike from the Tower of London. Some of these were re-issued during the Civil Wars. VII.815

Pike heads could be made by skilled cutlers, but many were churned out in their hundreds by local blacksmiths, such as those based in the ironworking regions of Shropshire and the West Midlands. Many pike heads took the form of a flattened diamond or lozenge, sometimes with an additional reinforced point. This design found favour with some military writers, like the Earl of Orrery, 'because they are sharp to enter, and when entered, broad to wound with'. Another type of pike head took the form of a long tapering blade with a flattened diamond cross-section, possibly the style being referred to in the 1639 'Direction for Musters' as 'sword-pointed'.

Pike heads, feet and staves were often produced independently before being assembled by pike makers. In April 1651 the Council of State paid £100 15s for 1,990 pike heads and feet to be packed in ten cases for transport to Ireland, whilst at Nottingham pike heads and staves were brought separately to the castle for assembly. Although gunpowder weapons had long eclipsed the bow on the battlefield, communities of bowyers still existed in 17th-century Britain and with their craft in decline many were forced to diversify. In producing pike staves, they were able to utilise many of their existing woodworking skills. Pikes were also supplied to both sides in considerable numbers from the Continent: between August 1642 and April 1645, roughly 16,000 pikes were exported to Britain. However, due to their length, conventional pikes, sometimes termed 'long pikes', were not suitable for every enterprise. Indeed, by the end of the wars in Ireland in 1652 few English soldiers carried them. Most campaigning by this time focused around sieges and skirmishes over difficult terrain for which speed, manoeuvrability and loose-order fighting were key. As a result, short or half pikes were also issued to both sides.

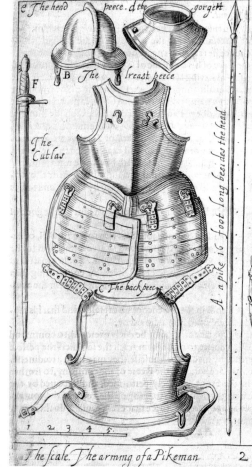

▶ Pikemen's equipment as depicted in Henry Hexham's *Principles of the Art Military* (1637).

Developed into a formidable fighting weapon by the Swiss during the Middle Ages, by the time of the Civil Wars the use of the halberd on the battlefield was largely confined to sergeants whose duty was to train and direct the men under their command. As such, Parliamentarian Richard Elton recommended the halberd as a useful weapon, as 'perceiving any Souldier out of order, he may cast in his Halbert between their Rankes, to cause him to march even abrest'. In addition to being the badge of rank of a sergeant, halberds were frequently used by personal bodyguards. In September 1642, for example, the Earl of Essex provided his guard with 30 halberds for £30, a considerable expense most likely reflecting the addition of etched and gilt decoration. By contrast, Sir John Pickering's Parliamentarian regiment was issued with 20 halberds for only £6 in 1645.

Much like half-pikes, halberds were also useful weapons when fighting in confined spaces or in skirmishing. As such, following the 'new-modelling' of the Scottish Covenanting Army in 1647, each new regiment was required to field 72 halberdiers who, in conjunction with musketeers, were to act in advance of the main force as a forlorn hope.

During the later 1500s and well into the next century, the halberd took on a wide variety of forms based on the same fundamental design. A convex or concave axe blade was balanced by a beak or fluke that was in turn surmounted by a long blade or spike. 17th-century halberd blades frequently incorporated pierced or open-work decoration, whilst others featured solid blades with cusped and hooked edges.

The partizan first appeared in the 15th century and despite its apparent practicality as a fighting weapon, it quickly became popular as a parade weapon and a badge of rank on the battlefield. Whilst Francis Markham described partizans in 1622 as being the weapons of both captains and lieutenants, by the time of the Civil Wars only lieutenants made regular use of them. The partizan consisted of a long tapering double-edged blade with two projecting flukes at its base, which Markham stated should be 'not above twelve inches of blade, sharpe and well steeled'. In April 1642 London suppliers quoted 14s for plain white (that is, plain steel) partizans, with an additional 2s 6d for tassels.

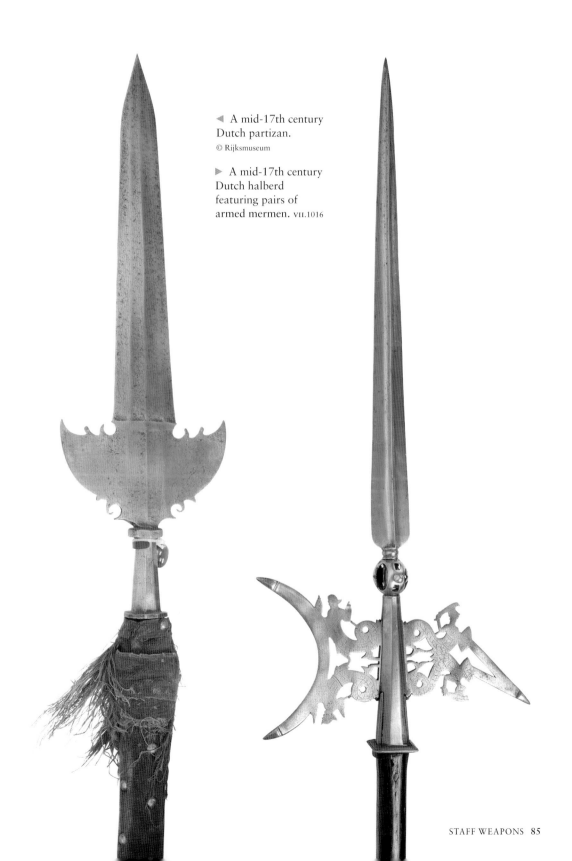

◀ A mid-17th century Dutch partizan.
© Rijksmuseum

▶ A mid-17th century Dutch halberd featuring pairs of armed mermen. VII.1016

By the mid 17th century, many infantry captains chose to arm themselves with 'leading staffs' instead of partizans. Though not technically a weapon, the captain's leading staff (sometimes termed a 'spontoon') may have developed in the late 16th century from the half pike or the boar-spear. Francis Markham was critical of their use in preference to the partizan, viewing them in 1622 as 'not fit to fight withal'. Many staff heads were highly decorated with ornate open-work incorporating human figures, animals and foliate designs.

Like pikes, halberds, partizans and other staff weapons were produced by many of the same craftsmen. Both the King's Pikemaker, John Edwards, and Yeoman of the King's Tiltstaves, Robert Thacker, made halberds and partizans alongside short and long pikes. Others, like Oxfordshire joiner David Woodfield, concentrated on the production of halberds. Both weapons were also imported from the Continent. In 1639, the merchant John Quarles supplied 107 partizans from the Low Countries, whilst in 1640 John Russell, who was purchasing arms for Strafford's troops in Ireland, was granted an export licence for 30 partisans and 50 halberds.

▶ Captain's leading staff with pierced decoration in the form of an officer. VII.229

POLLAXES AND BILLS

Although regarded as being medieval weapons, pollaxes/poleaxes and bills continued to be used during the Civil Wars, chiefly by the Royalists who remained chronically short of equipment. Both long and short pollaxes were issued during the wars, the former mainly to those soldiers who lacked more conventional weaponry. In May 1643, a survey of the Royalist stores in Oxford listed 750 long pollaxes together with a large quantity of bills and halberds. Many of these would have been obtained from local blacksmiths and ironworkers with experience of producing rudimentary but effective pollaxes to slaughter cattle. More elaborate long pollaxes were also used by officers and guardsmen as an alternative to other staff weapons such as leading staffs or halberds.

▲ Prince Rupert carrying a horseman's pollaxe on the frontispiece of this Parliamentarian tract.

Cavalry appear to have made wide use of the short pollaxe, as an effective close-quarter battle axe. In his 1644 treatise *The Young Horseman* John Vernon advised that the harquebusiers should carry a pollaxe particularly when facing well-armoured cuirassiers. At the battle of Edgehill, for example, a Parliamentarian cuirassier withstood a sword blow but was killed by a pollaxe wielded by one of the king's Gentlemen Pensioners. Notably, a rare and highly informative description of a contemporary pollaxe as used by the Gentlemen Pensioners was given by Sir Edward Southcote: he described his father using 'his little battleaxe, a weapon all the King's troop made use of … It was very like the masons lathing hammers, and had a sharp little axe on one side, and a hammer on the other'.

Parliamentarians too made use of the pollaxe. In his memoirs, the Royalist Sir Richard Bulstrode wrote how he had nearly been killed by a pollaxe at Edgehill, only to be saved by a comrade who shot the assailant dead with his pistol.

Other than the long pike, the most common staff weapon used by the Royalists was the 'black' or 'brown' bill. Whilst accounts of the time appear to have regarded them as two different types, their precise distinction is no longer clear. According to Randall Holmes' 'Academy of Armory' (1688), black bills appear to be synonymous with 'hedging bills': 'The Black bill, or Hedging bill, is an Instrument used both in warre, and also in domestick affaires, by Labourers and husbandmen, and by reason thereof, is generally knowne by the name of an hedging bill … and in warre is termed, a black bill'. Unfortunately, there are no similar indications as to the characteristics of the brown bill.

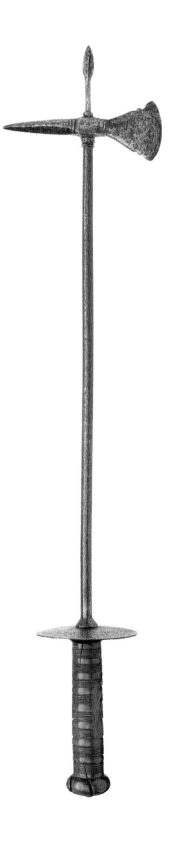

▶ Short cavalryman's pollaxe, first half of the 17th century. VIII.98

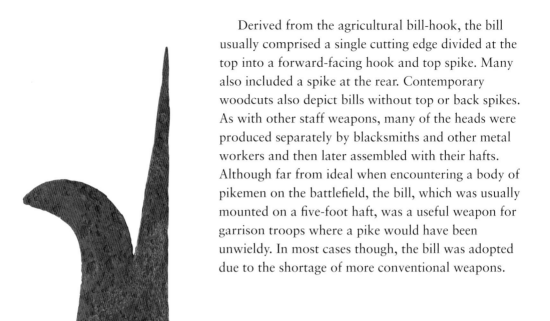

Derived from the agricultural bill-hook, the bill usually comprised a single cutting edge divided at the top into a forward-facing hook and top spike. Many also included a spike at the rear. Contemporary woodcuts also depict bills without top or back spikes. As with other staff weapons, many of the heads were produced separately by blacksmiths and other metal workers and then later assembled with their hafts. Although far from ideal when encountering a body of pikemen on the battlefield, the bill, which was usually mounted on a five-foot haft, was a useful weapon for garrison troops where a pike would have been unwieldy. In most cases though, the bill was adopted due to the shortage of more conventional weapons.

▲ 17th-century bill head from Farleigh Hungerford Castle, Somerset. VII.1816

▶ Royalists carrying a variety of staff weapons including halberds and numerous different types of bill.
© British Library

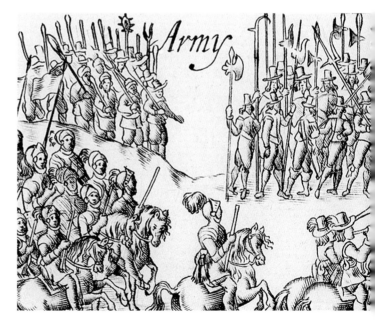

In August 1643, after the founding of the Solemn League and Covenant, the Scottish Convention of Estates issued a 'Proclamation for putting the nation in a posture of defence'. Amongst its various points the articles specified the arming of troops which conceded that men unable to find muskets or pikes could instead 'be furnisched with halbert, lochwaber axes or Jedburgh staffes'. Unfortunately, despite being relatively widely known today, their precise 17th-century form is difficult to establish. According to one Scottish dictionary of the time, the blade of a Lochaber axe was said to resemble the long tapering peninsular of the Rhins of Galloway. Certainly by the 17th century the name 'Lochaber axe' appears to refer to a long hafted weapon with an axe head longer than it was broad, with a gently-curved cutting edge and a separate hook projecting from the top of the staff. The precise function of the hook is unknown but it could have been used as an aid in scaling walls or pulling down fascines. To make matters more confusing it is clear from the records of the Scottish Privy Council that the term 'pollaxe' was interchangeable with Lochaber axe.

Published in 1521, John Major's *History of Greater Britain* noted that the blacksmiths of Jedburgh made weapons consisting of four-foot blades set on a stout staff. Although more problematic to identify than Lochaber axes, the Jedburgh staff may refer to those weapons which incorporated a long narrow tapering blade which extended beyond the top of the wooden haft. In the burgh records of Edinburgh in 1548 a Jedburgh stave was said to be the Scottish name for what the French termed a light horseman's spear – suggesting that unlike the Lochaber axe which was more suited to cutting, the Jedburgh stave was a particularly good thrusting weapon.

▶ Lochaber axe, 18th century. VII.873

LANCES

Although lancers were still recorded on muster lists of the Trained Bands as late as 1639, the use of the heavy lance in English armies had long fallen out of use. Whilst contemporary cavalry manuals continued to include sections on the arming and training of lancers, the Earl of Orrery acknowledged that 'I look on the Lance now as wholly laid by, and I think, with reason; for the Lance does little, unless it be by the force of the Horse's Course, or Carreer'. In contrast the lighter lance, otherwise known as a horseman's staff, continued to be used in Scotland and the Borders.
Two months after the invasion of Scotland by Oliver Cromwell in 1650, for instance, John Colquhoune of Glasgow produced 600 lances for the Scottish army. Unlike the heavier tapered and fluted lance, the horseman's staff was essentially a spear much like a shortened pike. Scottish lancers proved their effectiveness at the battle of Marston Moor (1644) when under the Earl of Balgonie they routed a Royalist infantry regiment, and in Ireland, which resulted in the Confederate leader Owen Roe O'Neil equipping one troop in each of his regiments of horse with lances.

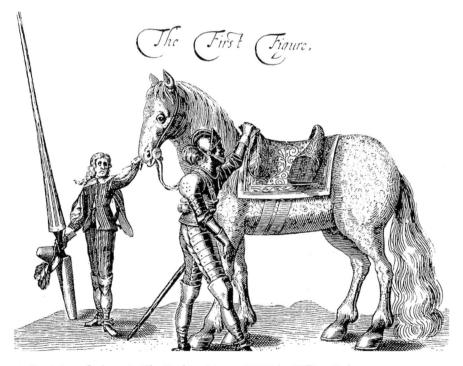

▲ Depiction of a lance in *The Vaulting Master* (1652) by William Stokes.

CONCLUSION

By the time Oliver Cromwell was declared Lord Protector of the Commonwealth in 1653, the Civil Wars had transformed Britain. It has been estimated that around half a million people lost their lives due to the conflict, the majority (around 300,000) in Ireland. Most died from accidents and disease, but in England and Wales between 75,000 and 85,000 were killed in battle. The material cost was also severe. Property worth millions of pounds had been damaged, the scars still visible in the landscape today.

The Civil Wars also had a transformative effect on arms and armour and the nature of warfare. Armour had largely been rendered obsolete thanks to the increasing dominance of firearms and a shift in cavalry tactics. Musketeers armed with matchlock, and in some cases flintlock, muskets proved themselves to be more effective and versatile than the 'gentlemen of the pike', just as lightly-armed harquebusiers took the place of cuirassiers. With its control of the capital and access to long-established foreign and domestic markets, Parliament had a significant advantage over the Royalists and was able to equip its armies as required. Whilst this undoubtedly contributed to Cromwell's ultimate victory, the Royalists were close to triumph on a number of occasions and were often able to overcome their deficiencies in the field. Nonetheless, Parliament's sustained war effort resulted in the formation of a modern, well-equipped fighting force that in the following decades enabled Britain to establish herself as a new world power.

◀ Oliver Cromwell by Robert Walker. © National Portrait Gallery

GLOSSARY

Bore	The interior of a gun barrel, which has a constant diameter.
Buff Coat	An oil-tanned leather coat worn with or in place of plate armour.
Burgonet	Open-faced helmet with a peak and cheekpieces. Close burgonets resembled close-helmets but with the addition of a peak.
Butt	The rear part of a stock of a gun.
Cask/casque	A contemporary term for a helmet.
Close helmet	Helmet enclosing the entire head with a visor and one or two bevors pivoted at the same points at either side of the skull.
Corslet	Half armour worn by pikemen, comprising back and breastplate and a pair of tassets.
Cuirass	Defence for the body formed of the back and breastplate.
Gauntlet	Plate or leather defence for the hand and wrist. Some gauntlets extended to cover the forearm.
Gorget	Defence for the throat, usually formed of a front and rear plate.
Greave	Plate defence for the lower leg.
Morion	Open faced helmet with a high crest or comb and an upswept brim. Sometimes known as a 'comb morion'.
Lame	Overlapping plates of iron or steel forming a flexible defence.
Lance	Cavalry spear up to 12 feet long.
Lock	The ignition mechanism of a firearm, fixed to the side of the stock.
Pauldron	Plate shoulder defence.
Peascod	Exaggerated padded stomach which projected into a deep rounded point overhanging the waistline.
Pike	Slender long spear of around 15 to 17 feet in length used by infantry. Particularly effective when used against cavalry.
Poleyn	Plate defence for the knee.
Pollaxe/ poleaxe	Long- or short-hafted infantry or cavalry weapon with a combination axe or hammer-head, a rear spike ('fluke') and sometimes a top spike.
Pommel	The end of a sword or dagger grip designed to provide a better hold and improve balance. In firearms, the rounded end of a pistol.
Pott	A contemporary term for either a light open-faced cavalry helmet or a pikeman's helmet.
Quillons	The cross bar on the hilt of a sword.
Sabaton	Plate armour for the foot.
Stock	The structural component of a firearm and the means by which it is held.
Tassets	Plate defence for the upper thighs either made of numerous separate lames or of embossed solid plates.
Vambrace	Plate defence for the arm.
Zischägge	German term for a light open-faced cavalry helmet, frequently fitted with a single sliding nasal.

FURTHER READING

Barratt, J 2000 *Cavaliers. The Royalist Army at War 1642-1646*. Sutton Publishing

Blackmore, D 1990 *Arms & Armour of the English Civil Wars*. Royal Armouries

Blair, C (ed.) 1983 *Pollard's History of Firearms*. Country Life Books

Caldwell, D H 1979 *The Scottish Armoury*. William Blackwood

Dowen, K 2017 'Seventeenth-century buff coats and other military equipment', in Mould, Q (ed.), *Leather and Warfare: Attack, Defence and the Unexpected*. Royal Armouries

Edwards, P 2000 *Dealing in Death. The Arms Trade and the British Civil Wars, 1638-52*. Sutton Publishing

Haythornthwaite, P 1994 *The English Civil War 1642-1651. An Illustrated Military History*. Brockhampton Press

Kenyon, J and Ohlmeyer, J (eds.) 1998 *The Civil Wars. A Military History of England, Scotland and Ireland 1638-1660*. Oxford University Press

Norman, A V B 1980 *The Rapier and Small Sword 1460-1820*. Arms and Armour Press

Richardson, T 2004 *The London Armourers of the 17th century*. Royal Armouries

Richardson, T and Rimer, G 2012 *Littlecote: the English Civil War Armoury*. Royal Armouries

Roberts, K 2005 *Cromwell's War Machine, The New Model Army 1645-1660*. Pen & Sword

NOTES ON CURRENCY AND DATES

During the 17th century British currency was based on the pound sterling. Money was divided into pounds (£), shillings (*s*) and pence (*d*). There were 12 pennies to a shilling and 20 shillings to the pound.

Until 1752 the civil or legal year began on 25 March, not on 1 January. As such the execution of Charles I was recorded as being on 30 January 1648 (Old Style), whereas today this is usually shown as 30 January 1649 (New Style). In this book both Old Style and New Style dates have been given for events falling within this period, hence: 1642/3.

ACKNOWLEDGEMENTS

This book would not have been possible if it had not been for the help and guidance of many individuals over the years. Firstly my thanks goes to Dr Thom Richardson, Curator Emeritus at the Royal Armouries, and David Edge, Armourer and Head of Conservation at the Wallace Collection, for nurturing my interest in the subject, sharing so much of their extensive knowledge on the arms and armour of the period and supporting me throughout the project. Special thanks also to Robert Woosnam-Savage, Curator of Armour and Edged Weapons at the Royal Armouries, Jonathan Ferguson, Keeper of Firearms and Artillery at the Royal Armouries, and Graeme Rimer, Curator Emeritus at the Royal Armouries, for all their much needed help and guidance on 17th-century edged weapons and firearms. Thanks also to Royal Armouries Librarian Stuart Ivinson and Image Librarian Jacob Bishop for obtaining so many invaluable sources. At the National Civil War Centre my thanks to Glyn Hughs, Curator and Team Leader of Exhibitions and Collections, and Kevin Winter, Exhibitions and Collections Assistant, for cheerfully putting up with my numerous visits and demands on their time. Special thanks to Antonia Lovelace and Shona Rutherford-Edge for reading drafts of the manuscript and making many helpful changes and suggestions. For the amazing photography, thanks also to Jacob Bishop, Image Librarian at the Royal Armouries, and Gary Ombler. Finally my thanks to Dr Martyn Lawrence for making this publication possible and providing me with much needed support during episodes of 'writer's block'.

Published by Royal Armouries Museum, Armouries Drive, Leeds LS10 1LT, United Kingdom
www.royalarmouries.org
Copyright © 2019 Trustees of the Royal Armouries
Keith Dowen has asserted his right under the Copyright, Designs and Patent Act (1988) to be identified as the author of this book.
ISBN 978 0 94809 290 9
Edited by Martyn Lawrence
Designed by Graham Moores
Series designer Geraldine Mead
Lock illustrations on pages 47, 49, 51 and 58 by Graham Moores
Photography by Jacob Bishop and Gary Ombler
Printed by Page Bros Ltd, Norwich
10 9 8 7 6 5 4 3 2
A CIP record for this book is available from the British Library
Every effort has been made to trace the copyright holders of images, where applicable.
Any errors or omissions are unintentional, and the publisher will be pleased to insert any appropriate acknowledgements in future editions.